YOU COULD BE AT SEA DANCE HOSTING

The Handbook

By

vanLee Hughey

ISBN: 1-4107-7805-3 (e-book)
ISBN: 1-4107-7718-9 (Paperback)
ISBN: 1-4107-9855-0 (Dust Jacket)

This book is printed on acid free paper.

1stBooks - rev. 11/04/03

ACKNOWLEDGMENTS

I'm indebted to those close friends who challenged me to put pen to paper, and the marvelous author Dr O.J. Bryson for the inspiration to keep going in the right direction. Equally significant to me are Josephine Williams, Stacy Walker, and Stephanie James who tirelessly corrected the errors unseen by my eyes. A special thanks goes to Phyllis Zeno and Marge Kosher who introduced me to the marvelous activity discussed in these pages.

To my mother, Luree Hughey, for saying to me, "Just do it." - ie., send my application to be a dance host. It changed my life.

WHAT PEOPLE ARE SAYING ABOUT
The Dance Hosting Handbook

"As director of a dance group that has done more than 100 cruises with hosts that included vanLee Hughey, I find his book the ideal resource for host "wannabes." They can glean everything they need to know about hosting on these pages and should be sailing in no time."
-- Phyllis W. Zeno, Director, AAA Merry Widows

"If every dance host aboard ship followed the suggestions in vanLee Hughey's excellent guide, we ladies who love to dance would keep coming back for more!"
-- Josephine Williams, Dance Cruiser

"This is a must read book for all prospective dance hosts and even those currently hosting. I congratulate vanLee Hughey for a through job of providing the insight to properly hosting onboard a ship or at a resort."
-- Jim McCown, VP Social Dance, USABDA

"The best user friendly guide and self help manual ever, on how to Host at Sea and enjoy the journey. Let an experienced professional join you and make you feel knowledgeable and confident on your 'maiden voyage.'"
-- Victor Bardack, Screenwriter and Film Producer

CONTENTS

I. INTRODUCTION

So...you're a man who likes ballroom dancing. Maybe you've heard that one can sail the oceans or visit some of the finest resorts in the world in exchange for dancing with beautiful, single women. Yes, it's true! You can, just as I have since 1989, *if*∴The right answers to the *if*s are what you'll find in the next few pages.

Perhaps you're just discovering the dance-host activity. You may have just been invited on your first assignment. Maybe you've been hosting for years and are still waiting for someone to define what is actually expected of you and how to be successful. This book will answer those questions and many more. Regardless of your hosting or dancing experience, your ability to enjoy life within the framework of the answers to these questions (the *if*s) is the key to your successful involvement. Many gentlemen are competing for the few good opportunities in this business. Some are handsome, some are charmers, and some are great dancers. Don't be intimidated. One obnoxious blunder by one of these "lady killers" can make you—a moderately attractive, not so much a charmer, and only a casual dancer—far more attractive to the Cruise Director, and the company. If you want to be selected for these opportunities, I'll share the secrets with you.

For simplicity, the term "dance host(ing)," will be abbreviated to "host(ing)." Sorry ladies, but to date there are no "she" hosts. Why? As you'll see, it's the women (lots of them) who are ready, willing, and able to dance, and who often vacation unaccompanied. These ladies represent a significant part of the market for luxury resorts, floating or not.

Can this fantasy be true? Can it be fun? Right now I'm on one of the most revered luxury cruise ships in the world. The ocean liner has just left Sydney, Australia. Ahead are many exciting ports including Hong Kong, Yokohama, and Hawaii. Yes, I'm in one of those few good positions. Having lived life this way for over a decade now, with travels valued in the tens of thousands of dollars each year, my answers to those questions are yes and yes! It's not a fantasy. It's all real. For photos from my most recent assignment, visit: www.cuatsea.com/guests/lvh.

What exactly is it that a host does? Each section herein discusses in depth the various aspects of life at first rate resorts and aboard luxury cruise ships in that capacity. For the answers to make sense, it will be beneficial to understand a bit of the background about dance hosting in the cruise industry. The evolved role and function of the host apply equally to assignments in the finest resorts in the world. To help you become a successful part of this reputable business as fast as possible, let's see what the role and function of this unique gentleman is and how you get involved.

Chapter 1 - BACKGROUND

From early in its existence, the cruise industry has seen various forms of the host program. This has been especially on ships appealing to the wealthy, which have always carried many more unaccompanied women than men. The result of this imbalance was that often these women felt left out at functions where there was dancing or other social activities.

Early on, several cruise lines saw the benefit of addressing this situation by inviting single men to dance with this special group of ladies.

Delightful Group of Dancers

The men received a free cruise in exchange for dancing with unaccompanied women. Until recently, social contact was restricted principally to dance functions. Approaching the end of the 20th century, the industry saw the benefit of expanding the social function of these gentlemen. Concurrently, the host program was moved from a staff-like function and made a part of the guests' enrichment programs. With that change, the role of the host was refined and intended to improve the satisfaction all guests' experience, but particularly that of female guests over the age of 55 who are traveling alone.

This group of special women remains the focus of the host program. For them, hosts get to sail and dance on the seas of the world. Yet, the fact is that when these gentlemen accept an assignment with a cruise line, they act in the capacity of a **social** host for all the guests. On the luxury ships, passengers are referred to as "guests," as is the practice at the finest resorts.

The social function of the host assigned to a ship (or resort) is to meet and mingle with everyone to help achieve the feeling of graciousness that once characterized the finest vacation experiences. A host does this by making personable contact with as many of the individual guests as possible. His objective is to awaken in them an awareness of their significance, i.e., make them feel important! He's onboard to break the ice with everyone as a cruise begins and socialize with them throughout their cruise.

The ship's staff are often overworked by the demands for timely delivery of activities for the ship full of people. The host, in contrast, is there to welcome and get to know personally as many of the individuals as possible, not just a select few. In return, he can be traveling the world in the comfort of the finest luxury ships afloat with guest status. A good host, whether working for a ship or a group sponsored by a private travel agent, develops meaningful friendships with people from around the world as well as with many of the lady guests. He gets to do this while exploring the world and savoring the fulfillment that comes from making a visible difference in the vacation experience of many people.

As a respected part of a ship's guest services, the host program is expensive for the company. It's provided with the expectation that it will increase everyone's enjoyment from the personalized attention. The best hosts in the business take both the social and the dancing responsibilities seriously. This means dancing appropriately and energetically wherever scheduled ballroom dance music is being played on the ship. It also means being socially "on", with a positive constructive attitude toward everyone whenever he leaves his room.

The man who enjoys this role must be in good physical and mental health since there are no days off. Weeks of continuous

4

dancing and being "on" socially requires above-average endurance, both physically and emotionally. (Note the word **energetically** in the previous paragraph.)

What exactly is it that a host does? He spends weeks at a time in a near-fantasy world, enjoying some of the finest food and entertainment in elegant environments with lovely ladies, dancing every ballroom piece played, socializing with diplomacy and tact. For the gentleman with these cultured abilities or who is willing to develop them, in addition to his above average skill as a dancer, this activity provides one of the most rewarding opportunities on the planet.

Chapter 2 - PEOPLE PLEASER

My introduction to hosting started with perhaps the best organized private dance/travel group that has ever existed. It is sponsored by a major travel agency and is still going strong after more than twenty-five years and over 125 well-applauded trips. I had flown into New Orleans and boarded a bus where there were 30 ladies from the demographic mentioned previously. Along with five other gentlemen, we spent that night dancing at a cajun style club emphasizing ballroom music, and then seven more nights dancing on a boat up and down the Mississippi River. The dancing I was ready for. The trouble was that no one had taken the time to tell me about the social responsibilities that went with the job.

Being somewhat of an introvert, with no social training to speak of, this was the first *if* for me. How about you? Are you typically cheerful? Do people, couples and singles, young and old, see you as outgoing? Would they say that you're a person with a positive attitude toward both life and those with whom you work? Can you comfortably spend a good deal of time engaging people (some you may not even like) in conversation—that means listening to them and guiding conversation—in a manner that brings out the positive in them? This last item, in practice, is perhaps the most challenging.

Listening and guiding conversation requires the expertise of an ambassador. Yet, it's one of the keys to success and a hallmark of the "best of the best" in this business. These men understand that the guests aren't there to listen to a host talk about his interests, opinions, or accomplishments. Bluntly stated, they don't want to hear him display or enhance his ego. Would you when you're paying the bill? Many gentlemen have been shown the way out for poor use of this and related social skills. That's why we're going to explore ways to excel in this interpersonal area. The section before that, however, will put us in the nightclub to talk about dancing.

Ships and the finest resorts used to be known for their warm, friendly atmosphere. That atmosphere is created by the staff and should be noticeable. Sadly, it has faded over the past decade until it's virtually gone from all but the finest cruise lines and establishments. This is a result of the staff's failure to perform its social functions.

The solution lies with the individual employee's training. Knowing what to do and actually doing it independently produces the desired results. The host is seen by the private travel agent or the ships senior staff as one of these well-trained individuals.

Think for a moment about ships. Every seven to twelve days, a ship begins a new cruise. Each cruise begins with several hundred to several thousand strangers. Of course, the magnitude of this guest changeover isn't nearly as great in the resort world. In either case, the guests have just arrived in totally new surroundings. The host is expected to take the initiative in greeting all the guests, and helping them to feel welcome, like he would in his own home.

In this business, **you** are that host. From experience, I can assure you that it's possible to make each guest you encounter genuinely feel that she or he is significant, that all of the staff is glad they have chosen this vacation, and that you look forward to sharing the experience with them. Chapter 8 will show you ways to sharpen your ability to do those things, both on and off the dance floor.

An important word to the wise: a lot of women traveling alone discovered the host programs years ago. Many choose a cruise vacation because of its host program. This group knows what the gentleman's role is and what he's expected to do. They've met hosts in the past, have had fun with them, and are looking forward to your getting to know them. Later, you'll learn about the importance of finding out who these particular ladies are when you're working for the ship. If you treat them, and all of the others who dance, as special friends or important associates, you'll do well.

Chapter 3 - NIGHTCLUB DANCER

Boarding that bus in New Orleans on my first assignment, I felt ready for the dancing. Thank goodness it was an eight-night trip because my first three nights were a disaster! I didn't seem to be able to lead, and several weren't following even the basic patterns. In time, it became clear that most of the ladies have major trouble on the dance floor until about the third night. Why? The only time many danced was on these trips, maybe twice a year. Yet, there were several who were active and good studio trained ballroom dancers.

Hence, the second important *if*: How is your danceability? Are you a **competent** social nightclub/ballroom dancer? Until you are, do not apply to be a host, since they are expected to be good dancers - see section II.

An Evening Begins

Hosts are primarily on board to dance every dance played by the band during the scheduled dance events with the unaccompanied ladies. Dancing will take three to four hours of his day. Making this part of the guest activities a satisfying one is what the organization and the ladies expect from the host.

Can you quickly recognize a lady's danceability? Can you limit or expand how you dance to match her ability? Can you properly lead a variety of ladies through an assortment of patterns in at least the six major dances and do it energetically? Can you name six of the primary American style ballroom dances? Is there some reason I specify the American style? Chapter 5 has the answers. Your accurate response to these last two questions will help you evaluate your competence.

Each host **must** be able to recognize and dance each of the major ballroom dances properly in a nightclub setting. That means he recognizes a piece of music as a tango and dances it as an American tango, a waltz is an American waltz, etc. Additionally, he must have enough experience on the dance floor to be able to adjust his dancing to the comfort level of each lady. This is nothing new—throughout the real dance world, it's the man's responsibility to help make the lady comfortable and feel that **she** looks good. That becomes a rule when one is hired to dance with the guests. To be among the best hosts working the world, one must be sensitive to each lady, be able to move properly with animation and dance her effectively.

Lessons and instruction from competent coaches should be part of each host's background and ongoing development. That helps produce the skill necessary to work with the range of abilities possible in a group of ladies. In addition to wanting to be asked to dance frequently and fairly, the ladies also want to be assured that they won't be embarrassed by their dancing. Typically, they'll expect the man to properly invite them to dance, escort them back to their seats, and be fair to all present. There is no expectation that a host's dancing be showy. Dancing with theatrical flare may frighten some of these women unless the host has demonstrated the ability to make every woman comfortable dancing at her level. He must dance each piece energetically, effectively for his partner, and with confidence. On the other hand, some women live for the opportunity and have the ability to be showy, which requires different skills from a host. Chapter 6 will address the issues of dancing in detail.

Here's an example of what doesn't work and why. Recently, a host spent an entire cruise dancing only occasionally, and then almost exclusively with a younger woman and a charming, attractive older lady. After the cruise, the attractive older lady commented negatively about this host's behavior. She and many others had noticed what he'd been doing, as they always do. Note: as a host you'll always stand out and be visible for everyone to see. The older lady mentioned a future assignment this man thought he had on a more elite cruise line later in the year to a member of that other line's host selection staff. Oops! There are reasons hosts disappear from the scene. You see, the older lady and several of her ignored friends book cruises and know dance programs on various lines. Let me elaborate on why such host behavior doesn't work.

The ladies watch everyone. After a pre-dinner dance set one night, two different ladies observed that "Nyla" danced every dance while our two ladies sat out almost a third of the time. A couple of hosts were playing favorites. The ladies noticed, and knew by name the hosts who got around equally to everyone. These ladies are not complainers. However, like everyone present, they expect each host in attendance to rotate equitably among **all** the ladies, and dance all of the dances properly. When a host doesn't, look out. He won't be back. There are several other specific social skills that are essential for survival and success. They'll be discussed in chapters 7 through 11.

The activity is truly easy and fun for the host who actually knows what he's doing on the dance floor, and is sensitive and fair to everyone - guests, hosts, and staff. If, as you complete this book, you do not support these dance responsibilities or social skills, don't apply for a host position.

Chapter 4 - BEING A TEAM PLAYER

Group of Hosts

Typically, there will be several hosts onboard at a time. Hence, the next *if* is: Are you able to interact and work with a group of guys as an equal, supportive team player? That doesn't necessarily mean socializing or even associating with them. Those are activities to be shared with the guests. However, it does mean getting along with your fellow hosts both socially and on the dance floor without hostility or envy.

Hosting is **not** the arena for self-centered, competitive/aggressive, or inflated ego behavior. Such inappropriate attitudes are expressed in many ways—arriving late for an assignment, sitting out a dance, criticizing other hosts, over-dancing the ability of the lady or space available, and inconsiderately interrupting a couple to ask the lady to dance.

Each dance venue is where members of a good team work together. They make sure that the least capable or most unattractive lady gets an equal number of pleasurable dances during each event.

vanLee Hughey

These are the places where each host arrives a bit early, ready and able to do his share of the dancing. That's done in a way that shows respect and consideration for the other guests and the other hosts.

SUMMARY

Can you picture yourself trading your enjoyment of nightclub dancing with splendid ladies for some incredible adventures sailing the oceans of the world? How do you feel about all the *ifs*?

1. Are you a cheerful, outgoing person with a positive orientation toward life? Can you comfortably spend a good deal of time engaging people in conversation? That is: listening to them and guiding conversation in a manner that brings out the positive in people while inviting them to have fun?
2. Are you a competent social nightclub dancer who can quickly recognize a lady's danceability, limit or expand your own competence to match hers, and, energetically lead her properly through at least the major dances?
3. Are you able to interact and work with a group of guys as an equal and supportive team player, even if they don't dress or dance as you do?

Are you ready to get into the details and mechanics to pursue this vocation? If you're already a host, are you set to improve your ratings and enjoyment of hosting? Specific guidelines for developing or improving the various capabilities you need to perform as a host are grouped in segments and presented in each of the remaining sections.

vanLee Hughey

II. DANCING AS A HOST

You'll recall that boarding the bus in New Orleans for my first assignment, I thought I was ready for the dancing. Was I ever surprised by the ladies' reactions and the skills needed to survive an evening of dancing with them. A few discoveries from those experiences that will help you to make your way through this mine field are included in the following chapters. This section shares those basic things that a host needs to know and be able to do as a dancer.

First and foremost, remember: hosts are aboard the ship to dance each and every piece of ballroom music played by the band with the unaccompanied ladies in attendance during the scheduled dance events. The ladies attending these events wish to make dancing a memorable time, every time. Hence, the dance floor is not the place to correct the lady or socialize with others. Hosts are not there to teach anyone or to tell them how to be better dancers by his criteria. That's the role of the dance instructors, for whom the ladies request and pay for this qualified guidance. How would you like to be the one who just wants to have fun dancing for a while and finds that each partner corrects your frame, position, footwork, or this or that? Which man was right? Ladies enjoy being competently led through material that's new to them, but within their "danceability." That skill as a dancer will clearly identify you as the best of hosts.

The forthcoming book *You'd Be Arrested If You Weren't On The Dance Floor* provides and teaches the wide range of knowledge a dance host needs to know. It's the complete "how to" manual for becoming a good nightclub dancer and dance host. In addition to discussing the transition from barroom and nightclub to ballroom dancing, it includes studio-like instruction on how to do the basic steps that hosts need in each of the dances. Hosts should understand that book's contents and the application of the concepts in addition to being able to properly perform all the steps presented. That knowledge, however you get it, is the prerequisite for being hired and remaining a host.

The way a host works the room and dances the floor while using all of the social skills discussed in the next section will determine his success in the eyes of the onlookers as well as by the ladies who are dancing.

Chapter 5 - DANCING FUNDAMENTALS

Hosts are most often thought of as American style social dancers. The world of partnership dance is made up of two schools—the American and the International. Within each of these schools there are two categories of dance—the smooth dances and the rhythm dances.

The Smooth Dances	*The Rhythm Dances*	
Foxtrot	**Cha-Cha**	**Rumba**
Waltz	**Samba**	**Mambo / Salsa**
Tango	**Swing**	

For those who've danced a good bit, this breakdown may seem simplistic. Watching people dance in various places, it may appear that there are as many ways of doing these dances as there are people doing them. The array of styles come from the different schools, or lack of training, and have evolved through both competitions and cross-cultural enjoyment of the activity around the world. The truth is that there are a limited number of commonly recognized steps, patterns and ways they're to be danced in the social/nightclub environment of the host.

The dances listed and terminology I use are from the American school. Nearly all people in the United States have learned the social style of ballroom dance from this school. It's adequate to satisfy their desires to dance and will meet the needs of a host. The social side of ballroom dancing is an easy place to start for those just getting interested in the activity as well as for those who only dance occasionally. Newcomers to dance begin with basic, or bronze, material and advance to silver and then gold level work. The complexity of patterns, body, and arm movements in each of the dances increases in divisions within each of these levels.

The ability to properly walk and lead a partner through a variety of patterns in at least all of the above dances effectively at the bronze level is the minimal expected background and level of proficiency for the vast majority of host assignments. These assignments normally involve working for private travel agents or companies targeting the

American market. Most of the ladies with International dance background are quickly able to follow well-led, basic American patterns. Only those gentlemen working the European market would need equal proficiency with the International style of dancing.

The International school of ballroom dancing has been well-established worldwide for a long time. In fact, its precision and energetic performance in Europe has been enough to establish this level of dancing as a sport for some time, so much so that its competition dance is now recognized as an Olympic event. Obviously, this is not the school for the fun loving, social dancer.

Hosts who come from the barroom-nightclub scene have spent the time needed to perfect their danceability in ballroom dance studios. This transition and the dance-related issues and problems hosts frequently encounter are addressed in training-like detail in my book *You'd Be Arrested If You Weren't On The Dance Floor*. It also includes detailed studio-like instructions on how to actually do and lead the required basic steps and patterns.

The atmosphere in which hosts spend their time is like, but much classier than, that of a local nightclub with a live band. It is not related to that of a dance studio or competition hall. Hence, proper dance etiquette, rather than ballroom styling, is even more significant and visible. One of my coaches likened the social nightclub scene to a diplomatic enclave. Rudeness and bad manners are simply not tolerated. This is especially true of a host. Everyone who attends one of our dances is there to have fun. They're not there to be instructed or made to feel less than perfect. Their minds are geared toward playing among the stars. The host's role is to be able to make the ladies feel relaxed and important as he dances properly with them. **Properly** means: if you choose to do a foxtrot, it's danced as a foxtrot, a rumba as a rumba, etc.

Each evening, the hosts are expected to create a social atmosphere that brings out the most rewarding behavior from the ladies and other couples present. In the facilities where hosts work, the majority of people enjoy dressing up for an evening of fun and fleeting romance on the dance floor. If the host dances well, uses common courtesy and demonstrates respect for others, he's bound to get on well in the social dance environment.

Loud, boisterous, and jealous behavior is frowned upon at any dance and especially from a host. Behavior related to barroom brawls is definitely out of place, as is improper use of alcohol that creates unacceptable conduct. If you have a temper or comparable attitude that has to be expressed, don't become a host! Good hosts are naturally in control of their feelings and at peace with life. The best have learned to live at least the five social skills that will be discussed in chapter 8. These skills include channeling any hostile feelings a host may experience into the dance itself. This is a healthy way to release and express emotion while staying in everyone's good graces.

Chapter 6 - PARTNERSHIP DANCING

● Holding Each Other

Using the proper dance hold and frame for each of the patterns in all of the dances is the secret to skillful performance. An improper hold or position 1) impedes the ability to lead the lady properly, 2) can throw a partner or couple off balance, and 3) contributes to creating an awkward appearance. Dancing in a hosts social nightclub setting doesn't dictate all the detail found in a ballroom studio. However, knowledge of frame, its construction and body positioning is indispensable for the host.

Frame refers to the posture and positioning of the upper and lower arms and the hands which define the way the couple holds each other while doing a dance. Once this initial dance position (hold) is set, the torso remains erect with the upper arms braced to it forming a toned unit - the frame. Essentially, the upper arms don't move independently from the torso during the dance. Rather, the entire unit moves as one to guide or lead the lady.

Closed dance position and hold, gentlemen, should conform to your partner's body structure, ie., physical characteristics of height and weight, and the dance being done. Body position and hold will also vary according to the dancers' experience. Typically,

Closed Dance Position - Open

in the smooth dances, the couple will hold each other something like these two figures. Many experienced ladies will often be more comfortable when dancing with an accomplished partner in a more compressed hold as shown here.

Closed Dance Position - Compressed

When the man's closed dance frame is constructed and the lady properly positioned, she will be able to maintain her position offset to his right side while being led through patterns and around the dance floor. Care must be taken not to let this off-center position become too pronounced, but the most common problem is finding the lady too directly in front of her partner. This off-center position will help ensure that both partners avoid stepping on each other's feet. If the man finds himself stepping on the lady's feet, or she is on his, odds are that he's pushed or allowed her to move directly in front of him. Effective arm and hand positioning (frame) by the man give him the ability to help place the lady properly to his right side.

● **Movement**

In order for a man to lead and relate well to any partner, it is essential that he know 1) what to dance to the music being played, 2) how that dance should look and be done, and 3) the precise execution of his patterns. The man must learn and be able to dance each pattern for all of the dances independently before he learns to lead them.

On the dance floor, his role is to lead his partner smoothly through each of the patterns that he chooses by using the proper footwork, frame and body position. To do that, he must be able to dance each pattern in time with the music while 1) maintaining balance, poise and posture; 2) using the proper foot, body, hand and arm-work; and 3) properly indicating to his partner the direction and rhythm he plans to take next.

The man should understand how to use the floor for each dance while leading each new pattern comfortably. That includes progressing down the Line of Dance (LOD) in all smooth dances while avoiding collision with other dancers on the floor. When he does one of the rhythm dances, he should be able to dance in a comparatively small area while executing turns and other open work in a manner that avoids colliding with other dancers. As these skills become natural, he then starts adding appropriate animation which is an important ingredient in appearance.

● **Dancing Up or Down to a Partner's Ability**
The next ingredient is the man's ability to determine what each partner is able to do. It's bad manners to expect a lady to perform a pattern that is beyond her skill or his ability to lead well. As soon as a host begins dancing with a partner, he takes responsibility to adjust to her danceability. With experience he can generally make that judgment accurately in the first few steps. When dancing with a newcomer the first few times, a host should begin with the basics to determine her balance and level of ability. Only after those few steps are done successfully, and with reasonable certainty established in his mind, should he attempt to gradually move onto more advanced movements.

Be cautious about dancing too closely, although proper compressed positioning is appropriate. As with the patterns, the lady will almost always indicate what hold she's comfortable with. Watch your hands! If a lady is uncomfortable with any of these aspects, and the problems go uncorrected, the negative result will show up on her quality evaluation form at the end of her vacation.

The point is that it's important for hosts to have above-average sensitivity and care for each partner's feelings to avoid embarrassing her. My sympathy and admiration go to the lady! She's doing

22

everything she can to dance successfully with each man, which is a major feat most of the time, gentlemen. It's a feat because every man dances the same rhythm differently. She's doing her darndest to figure out what it is he wants her to do even if he's dancing a waltz to the foxtrot the band is playing. A host is expected to know what is what and why he's doing it.

By the way, just because she did a pattern well last night, doesn't mean she's with it tonight. The same rules of accommodation apply here too. The host who consistently helps each lady feel good about her dancing will be greatly respected for his sensitivity and recognized as a good dancer. It's not what moves the man is able to do that matters, but rather what the lady is able to do comfortably with him. A host should be able to feel that combination quickly with every woman with whom he dances. Tonight, my partner for a mambo was a tall lady in her late seventies with poor balance and uncertain footing. Having accepted the invitation to dance, she asked "What is this?" just after the band leader said "...and here's a mambo." "Something with some swing in it," was my response, to which I felt her relax. She did her best and felt great after getting through a good single step swing. Let me say it again. It's not how magnificently the man can dance the rhythms being played that matters, but what the lady is able to do comfortably when she's his partner.

● **The Invitation**
Recently, an elegant lady on a world cruise complained that she and other ladies' were being offended by belittling invitations to dance. Why does it happen? Beyond lack of knowledge and sensitivity, often ineffective hosts compensate for their insecurity by displaying an inflated ego. This comes across as a condescending attitude to some ladies. These hosts say things like, "Well, it's your turn to dance. Let's go." That shows no respect for anyone and does not help the lady feel important.

The correct method is, with a compassionate attitude, a gentleman asks a lady for a dance by approaching her comfortably. He gently extends his hand toward her with a slight bow and politely says something like, "Hello, I'm Bert. Would you like to do this dance with me?" The lady then has a choice.

The process is slightly simpler with ladies with whom a rapport has developed, but a considerate invitation should still be extended. Corny? Assuredly, yet when done with the attitude and grace of a gentleman, each of the pieces are automatic and in character. The process is recognized as appropriate by the well-bred ladies and the onlookers we travel with. Properly followed, it paves the way to less-formal interactions without offending anyone.

If the invitation to dance is refused, the host should accept the declination with dignity and move on to another prospective partner—again, with a smile. Make a point to return to these ladies with another invitation when the band is playing a piece with a totally different rhythm. Don't take a refusal personally. There are many reasons for refusing a dance, none of which should matter to the host. There are always others who'll be ready to dance.

- **Floorcraft**

While on the dance floor, the gentleman is **driving**. He must be just as aware of other dancers as he is of other cars on a two-way street to avoid colliding with them. This is often difficult when one is first learning a new dance. Many of the guest couples who'll be sharing the floor will be in this group. These newcomers can complicate floor work for even the most accomplished host. Still, he must adjust his dancing so it's done without bumping into other couples or obstacles. If a collision with another couple occurs, the host apologizes immediately regardless of who's at fault, and then goes on his way.

All dance patterns in the smooth dances are designed to

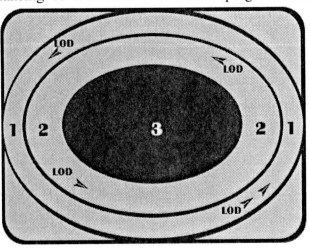

Dance Floor Divisions & Lines of Dance

24

move around the entire dance floor in a counter-clockwise direction in lanes 1 and 2. This direction is referred to as the line of dance (LOD). On the social dance floor of a ship or resort, you can expect that most couples will never have heard of this concept or other floorcraft courtesies. Hosts, however, should use them properly.

Honoring the division of the dance floor allows for various styles and types of dancing to be done during any given number. Couples should enjoy doing their thing toward the middle - 3 - of the dance floor, unless they're moving continuously around the perimeter at the same speed as others there. Lanes 1 and 2 are used by dancers traveling the Line of Dance (LOD) around the floor. The outside lane is left open for the fastest moving couples circling the floor. The inner-most part of the floor is for the dancers remaining more stationary and those doing patterns in place.

Latin and rhythm dances are typically danced in a small space referred to as a spot. For these dances, each couple picks a spot and confines most of their steps to its space. If there are a couple or two moving around the dance floor, let and expect them to use that outside lane - 1. Those who observe these simple courtesies are recognized as good dancers.

- **Focus/Attentiveness**

With floorcraft trained into the autonomic nervous system along with the patterns, the host can be totally attentive to the woman with whom he's dancing. When he has taken a partner to the floor, it's proper to focus his attention on her. Gentlemen who scatter their attention when dancing to recognize or talk to other women, or to horse around with other hosts are ignoring and discounting their partners. These men and women are considered rude and run the risk of appropriate criticism. For a host, this is his partner's three minutes of attention.

For the best of the best, each ballroom dance is an intimate interaction between him and his partner. The objective is to function together as a unit to the music being played. The closeness and synchronized movement can be a beautiful experience for both the couple and for those watching. This is the foundation for making the **magic** happen.

● **Closure**

After the dance has ended, as he escorts his partner back to her seat, the host thanks the lady and expresses his enjoyment of sharing the dance with her. This is the time to be using the well-polished skills of positive reinforcement that are discussed in chapter 8. I was honestly able to compliment my mambo partner (page 23) on her execution of the last underarm turn in our dance as "...the best she's done it on this trip." She knew the comment was true. On the opposite side of the fence, it's rude for a gentleman to walk off the dance floor leaving the lady on her own, and vice versa.

SUMMARY

The impression of an excellent dancer attributed to the best hosts comes from a depth of experience and good rhythm they've gained on the dance floor. Their floorcraft and styling appear natural. These hosts will typically dance over more of the floor, with the classical courtesy and good manners that are expected of all men on the dance floors in the world at large. Reaching that level of proficiency from the barroom or nightclub level of dancing means moving into the social ballroom scene.

vanLee Hughey

III. CHARACTERISTICS & EXPECTATIONS

A host on assignment for a resort or cruise line is neither a guest nor an employee. Further, he is purposely distanced from the staff since his role is to interact directly with the guests as individuals. He's the host to the people visiting his residence to help them get involved in the vacation they've chosen. He's there to help make everyone feel significant both on and off the dance floor.

Can you see yourself in the elegant surroundings of a ship at sea, dancing effectively, and being a conservative catalyst stimulating interaction among the people around you?

Looking back, I would have said, "That ain't me—I'm out of here!" But wait a minute. There's no need to panic. Remember that I was the one with few social skills or the information contained herein when boarding that bus loaded with ladies on our way to a week together. Bruised, having suffered too much unnecessary anguish hosting, and with some good encouragement along the way, I've made it. You can succeed at the activity a great deal more easily after digesting the contents of this book. The interpersonal part of the role, as opposed to the dancing side, really isn't difficult once you learn the steps, so to speak.

The man who can dance well and function as a friendly, refined gentleman is a unique commodity in today's hectic society. We've already painted a picture of the role this gentleman plays emphasizing the major components of that image—people pleaser, nightclub dancer, and team player. If the information on dance in the previous chapter was anything other than a review or if you were left with questions about how to do any of it, please refer to the book *You'd Be Arrested If You Weren't On The Dance Floor*.

Let's explore and discuss how to develop several of the other key attributes that produce the host who functions smoothly and successfully.

vanLee Hughey

Chapter 7 - ATTITUDE

Each host's own very personal attitude, more than anything else, will affect the results he experiences. Being aware of that simple fact is especially important as one ventures into this new undertaking. It's the most significant advice that can be understood by those wishing to succeed in this activity. Those who realize the impact their attitude has on what they see and how they react to the events in their life hour by hour, will be on the right path. That awareness will enable a host to:1) select those thoughts and make those choices, which will produce enjoyment throughout the days of an assignment; or 2) accept responsibility for the results of the thoughts and behavior he experiences. The attitude each host chooses will be the key to his gratification from socializing and dancing around the world. It's really an inside job!

A healthy personal attitude distinguishes the successful host from those who disappear or drop out along the way. A host reveals who he is by the way he conducts himself and by the way he relates to both those present and absent. Being inappropriately critical of someone not present tells those in attendance a lot about the speaker. Most guests will be onlookers, noticing the hosts' appearance and behavior, and listening to his conversations. When one of these people doesn't like what she sees or hears, she'll pass the word along. It's not uncommon for the observation to race through the entire facility and get back to the host before the end of the day.

Hosts are recognized by many folks they won't ever talk to - the onlookers. Those in the role of host are visible and very public. We hosts are living in a glass house with eyes watching and ears listening all the time. This is more true aboard a ship than at a resort. The good news is that hosts don't have to have problems with onlookers' impressions or reactions, or those of the ladies that dance.

Tonight, the seventh night of a long cruise, a new host told me of his disappointment and frustration with the disinterest a few of the ladies had in him and his dancing. They were obviously crazy about dancing with the most accomplished dancer among the hosts. His comparison of their behavior left him feeling dejected and inadequate.

At the same time he pointed out his lack of skill, experience and ability as a dancer.

It was commonly known that several of these ladies were already taking private lessons from the resident instructors on board to supplement their previous years of ballroom dance instruction. They were excited to find and dance with the accomplished host since he had the ability to rival the instructor they were studying with on the ship. He was also, perhaps, the most seasoned host in the company. Hence, he had both the interpersonal and dance skills to dance them at their advanced level of ability. He'd also traveled and danced with them previously, resulting in established camaraderie.

Beyond failing to heed the warning in chapter 3 about being a competent dancer before accepting an assignment, the upset host didn't understand the significance of his attitude or its impact on his perceptions and feelings. He had not developed to the point that he could see himself in the host's role safely and in context. As a result, he was asking the ladies to show him how to do steps and to move differently while upsetting himself in the resulting situations. Actually, he would have been doing an adequate job if he could just have accepted himself doing the best he could at the time while learning new and different things later.

There are several keys to an attitude which produces the internal feelings and external behaviors that result in social and interpersonal success as a host. The first is internalizing a clear image of the host's role.

The best hosts have the ability to truly leave life in the real world on the other side of the door that was closed just before departing for an assignment. A man cannot work positively through the challenges of hosting when part of him is screaming to be someplace else. A host fails to function well when thoughts of a lover, family, business or another place are active in his mind. No one can effectively tune into a conversation and hear what the other person means when his mind is busy processing other things. A host who's mind is elsewhere, often finds himself tilting with the windmills of his imagination rather than being aware of the potential of the moment. He, like the host above, neither enjoys nor is seen as competent in the position he's accepted.

Another of the keys to right thinking is to get rid of personal agendas, like latching onto some wealthy lady. A bit later we'll talk specifically about romance. I'm sure you can think of other agendas. Any of them will adversely affect a host's attitude and experience. Here are a few secrets that will help avoid those results while getting the best personal payoff from hosting.

A proper attitude yields a foundation that can be relied on for good, rewarding, and often surprising results over time. From simple acceptance of who one is, comes peace within himself. Then, 1) he can function with a secure, sensitive, compassionate view of others, and 2) take responsibility for his reactions to other people and events. With this point of view, a gentleman will be able to care about the enjoyment of other people and consider their comfort before his own in the role of a host. This sensitivity is the starting place. Those other people include the guests, hosts, enrichment people, and staff from housekeeping to the senior officers. It's the correct view of the world for the gentleman host.

With that foundation, these men are amongst the happiest people on any vacation. They enjoy their time, ask for what they want, and treasure what they're doing. These intangible rewards are part of the personal payoffs that go with the territory to those with the right attitude. The moment by moment behavior nurtured by that right thinking will effectively prevent problems from the ladies and the onlookers. It prevents the actions that produce unwanted reactions.

In the next chapter we'll look at specific steps in the process of developing and exercising this indispensable attitude, and the payoffs that come to those with that foundation. Without it, even hosts who are terrific dancers will frequently encounter a variety of emotionally upsetting situations. They will allow those situations to taint the rest of their perceptions and behavior, ruining an otherwise wonderful assignment and avocation.

Chapter 8 - SOCIAL SKILLS

Many years ago, Dale Carnegie provided a clear set of guidelines which, even today, actually help innumerable people relate effectively. Several of his basic rules define core behaviors demonstrated by a host's right thinking, i.e., attitude:

- ✦ Don't criticize, condemn, or complain.
- ✦ Do give honest, sincere appreciation.
- ✦ Do become genuinely interested in other people.
- ✦ Do smile.
- ✦ Do use a person's name accurately and often.

Understanding the purpose of and genuinely living by the principles which Mr. Carnegie discusses in *How to Win Friends and Influence People* provides a full ring of keys which are invaluable to any host. Don't accept an assignment until you've read that book. Each of the precepts that Mr. Carnegie discusses helps hatch the right thinking we've been talking about. However, until a person understands these principles clearly enough for them to become an integral part of his personality, the attempted use of them will be perceived by others as false and phony. Phony is the opposite of the persona hosts are onboard to create. As one develops the inner empathy for people outside himself, the effect of behaving in accordance with these rules will be very evident to everyone. That directly relates to preventing problems with those onlookers.

Be aware that simply reading through *How to Win Friends and Influence People,* or any other good book on the topic, will not produce a quick fix of a person's attitude. Until the significance of the people and the importance of dealing with them sincerely becomes ingrained and interwoven into the fabric of his personality, the overall role of host won't be played any more successfully than a man will be able to lead a lady through a complex tango step that he once saw someone do.

The best way to quickly develop that attitude is to simply start living with these five simple rules of socializing. The toughest rule is typically the first one. Just how does a person live life without criticizing, condemning, or complaining? The answer involves the interaction of their judgments, expectations and ego needs. It means paying attention to one's thinking minute by minute, and then fixing those "C" thoughts before they slip out of the mouth. As with repeating new dance patterns, this social process will become automatic. Eventually it evolves into part of an automatic orientation toward life. Getting these rules (the steps of the **social** dance) rooted into at least the role of a host will yield an attitude (internal) and behavior (external) that will produce unexpectedly positive results (payoff).

Those who visit the finest hotels and resorts or cruise on the few truly luxury ships still afloat, are impressed by and attracted to those employees who live these principles (the patterns they dance) as they deal with their guests hour by hour. Like those employees, the best of the best hosts are equally sincere and genuinely extend themselves to others. When hosts begin to care about other people their social clumsiness and self-consciousness fall away. That's when they begin experiencing personal enjoyment from interacting with the guests who are visiting their "home," sharing a short journey through life. The results often are priceless.

When our refined gentleman lives the right thinking of a host, what happens when he steps "out there?" For starters, realize that whenever a host is out of his room, he's seen in the role of a host. He's socially ON. To those around him, he doesn't have somewhere else to be or some other activity to attend to like all the rest of the staff.

Before "the best" walks out of his room, he reminds himself that he's ready to meet and deal with the people who make it possible for him to be living life like a prince. Meeting and dealing includes three things: 1) saying hello first, 2) seeing that everyone's enjoying their vacation, and 3) helping them feel comfortable and special.

To be one of them, relax into the role of an elegant gentleman creating a gracious environment helping even the staff to feel significant. Look in a mirror and smile, take some deep easy breaths, slow down, and open the door to leave the room. This little bit of preparation produces beneficial results throughout every assignment. With that, you're on!

Here are some specific behaviors that are part of your day as a host.

- **Take the initiative like a diplomat.**

You are the host here. They are the guests. People are flattered when they're recognized and greeted as special people. By your saying hello in that fashion and introducing yourself, they no longer need to feel like strangers in new surroundings.

Cool your jets! Introduce yourself, always with a warm smile. Tell them your name and add a five-second sound byte about what you do or where you live. Learn to use sound bytes that open the door for a response. Then help them take over the conversation. They have things that they want to talk about. How do you do all that?

Ask, get, and learn their name. If you don't do anything else, learn and use their name properly. If necessary, carry a small notebook to jot down names and keywords. Use it for recall when needed, but address them by name.

Ask about where they live. Someone else may be from the same area and you can get them together.

Ask about their family. By now a conversation may be flowing. Remember, let them show their pictures and talk about their family (period). This is NOT an opportunity for you, a host, to talk about yours. Can you see why I said earlier not to carry your personal life or problems out here?

Ask about their hobbies or interests. This is another area where it is wise to have a sound byte or two ready to stimulate and then redirect the conversation.

Ask about their other vacations and cruises. Have they visited this resort or sailed with this cruise line before? If the answer is yes, then they're in a group of people who are important to you because they're important to the company. They are repeaters. Surprise yourself by finding out how many times they've returned.

As the vacation progresses, ask if they're enjoying their vacation. When it's appropriate, ask if they enjoyed an activity they've just finished or the port you've just left.

As their vacation comes to an end, ask about their plans when they return home.

● **Be expressive and optimistic.**

Whenever you say "hi," do it in a manner that makes them feel like a significant friend. While I was working on this chapter, a guest performer caught my eye on several occasions while she'd been moving around the ship. Her expression and presence had been naturally magnetic to many of the guests. Everyone spoke highly of her though most hadn't even met her. She was a nice, although rather normal-appearing, lady. Yet, that right attitude was reflected in her facial expressions and demeanor which were animated and pleasant. People who haven't cultivated that personal attitude rarely attract that complimentary attention. With it, the individual comes across as sensitive, genuine, and tactful.

Whenever you're asked how you feel or how you're doing, the answer should always be the equivalent of, "Wonderful," and said with a smile. For example, "I'm splendid" or "I'm getting better," but be genuine. The ground rule here remains the same: never criticize, condemn, or complain. If you cannot say something good and positive as a host, you shouldn't be out around people. Sorry, but that's the business a host is in.

● **Focus on the other person.**

Here it comes again, because it's ignored by too many hosts. Just stop and relax so you can genuinely listen. Tune into the guest(s) and what they're saying, and not saying, instead of the thoughts that have wandered into your mind. Don't talk except to stimulate or guide the conversation. Nothing is more flattering than the rapt attention of another. The guests want you to hear what they've just done or what they just bought, and applaud them. They don't want you telling them.

Making eye contact while talking is important. Look at the other person with interest. How large are the pupils of their eyes? Eye contact is a great aid in listening to them and it will also keep you from thinking about other things while they're talking.

Simply learn to be interested. Magnetic people have that sincere, caring quality. They're able to see or ask how they can be helpful. React to what the other person is saying and how they say it. This will be natural when you're focused on them.

Before speaking, think about how your comments will help others feel significant. Don't make people self-conscious. We'll revisit this concept when we delve further into the dancing side of the host's role.

- **Display a sense of humor.**

   Great people maintain a positive sense of humor. Hosting exists to help guests have a more fulfilling holiday. That's not done with the seriousness of brain surgery or the championship dance finals at Blackpool. Vacationers like to be around people who make them feel good. They gravitate to those who help them relax and feel light-hearted.

   Lighten up. Adjust your attitude for a happy heart and mind. When you're feeling playful, it's much easier to spot things around you that are unintentionally funny. Using these observations and events is a lot more effective than prepared or contrived material.

   Carefully used self-effacing humor is another people pleaser. A likable friend of mine is an attorney who uses lawyer jokes very effectively. This includes occasionally aiming them at himself and laughing heartily at the punch line. Laughing at oneself shows he's down to earth and confident.

   Have a few good jokes or stories that you can tell well. Ensure the material is well-prepared and appropriate for the audience. Good observations, stories, or jokes can help create a light-hearted atmosphere that gives people encouragement to interact freely. As a host, you can set the pace by becoming an example of openness as you strive to make the guests shine by drawing them into the spotlight and reacting to what they have to say.

- **Praise and flatter others.**

   People crave attention, appreciation, and the resulting feeling of importance. Hosts are in exactly the role to provide that recognition. Notice the people around you, the work they do, how they look, how they dance, and then be generous in your praise. That, by the way, includes the other hosts. Feeling good about this recognition is why people pay their money to return to the particular luxury resort or cruise line.

Individualize compliments. Applaud something specific so your comments will be recognized as realistic. Be sure what you say is genuine. If folks don't feel there's sincerity behind what you say, they'll think you're a fraud. Warning: when people discover that you're praising and applauding several others in the same manner, your image can immediately revert to that of a con artist. Being generous with appropriate, well-deserved praise and flattery in the right place is a winning characteristic of the best.

One example of excellent flattery is finding the right opportunity to quote the other person. It shows that you feel they're special enough to actively listen to. "As you said so nicely last night..." is a form of recognition that everyone appreciates.

● **Make mistakes good.**

Hosts with a good attitude react confidently to the situations around them. They do what feels appropriate, which occasionally turns out to be wrong at that time. When things fail to turn out well, these men immediately apologize and do what they can to fix the situation. They don't go around putting themselves down. Good hosts carefully review the important and embarrassing events to see how and why they got into the mess, and the lesson(s) each contained. Remember that sense of humor we talked about? It's a great life-saver while making the way back to normal.

I made a dreadful mistake during pre-dinner dancing one evening. There were two ladies who always sat together waiting to dance. One often redirected my invitation to the other less-experienced lady. This evening, I didn't listen to the piece the band was starting to play and asked the first lady to dance. We started to the floor when I realized the number being played was one that I'd prefer dancing with the less-experienced woman since we'd been doing some skill development to the rhythm. The lady on my arm had asked me to dance with her friend under similar circumstances on several previous occasions. So, I asked if it would be appropriate for me to dance this one with her. She said sure, meant no, and was offended, as she should have been. I apologized on more than one occasion, but it was several days before we were dancing and having fun together again. Lesson learned: once you've asked a lady to dance, there is no turning back (period).

There's wisdom in keeping a diary or journal of the things that work and the things that got you into trouble. Learn from all your experiences and those of the other hosts.

● **Use names.**

The single most significant social truism is that a person's name is, to them, the sweetest and most important sound in any language. Becoming good at remembering individuals by name is one of the best social skills a host can develop. Make a conscious effort to shake hands and give your name to every guest onboard the ship, and then get their name. Have fun seeing how many you can remember accurately.

The Key: Before an introduction, look at the person and get your mind set to record and use their name. Then, listen and pay attention as the introduction begins, and use the name immediately afterwards. The real growth occurs through active, conscious practice. In the truly elegant environments around the world, addressing everyone as Mr./Mrs./Ms./Dr., and last name is applauded. Everybody on vacation is looking forward to making new friends. They're surrounded by opportunity and hosts help them get started. Hearing their name spoken and used properly stimulates the process.

Warning: Don't play games or be silly with people's names, and don't speak them incorrectly regardless of their origin. Names of people from various countries around the world may sound and feel strange, yet they are just as significant to their owners as the cruise director's or your own.

SUMMARY

Do not dominate conversations. Many good dancers and nice men have been eliminated from hosting programs for this one particular social flaw. Be genuine with comments. Be realistic when using flattery. These social techniques are skills that have proven very effective for hosts and staff who relate skillfully to their guests. The task of each host is to create the relaxed, cordial environment that has been lost in our fast and complex way of living today! Use these social skills to help enhance the vacation experiences and dreams of the guests.

The product of the resort and cruise industry is the fantasy world. When the host role is performed with sincerity and grace, these gentleman have the opportunity to help many people conceive exciting new dreams that will often brighten their life for years to come.

The nightclub dance floor is the perfect setting for a host to be the finest of dream weavers. Those men who help the guests enjoy their fantasies will be enriched beyond description. There is little that equals the value of guests, ladies and couples alike, who depart saying to a host, "You really made this a special trip for me...I hope to do it with you again, soon!" When they discover that man on another vacation even years later, their special recognition will be priceless to him.

Several of the keys both on and off the dance floor to helping each guest feel important is using their name, listening to them, recognizing them, and applauding their uniqueness, all done with the right attitude.

Chapter 9 - OVERALL HEALTH

In addition to having the social and dance skills necessary to be an effective host, a person must feel up to playing the role, day after day. Being in good emotional and physical condition is essential. Remaining rested is an art. Effective performance depends on having the energy and stamina needed to meet the demands of an evening of nonstop dancing after a day of socializing. As days blur into weeks, the benefits of resting often and sleeping well will become obvious. Beyond being physically and emotionally healthy, the best hosts learn to pace themselves. This process governs their choice of activities and the way they do what they do both day and night.

Physically, every dancer must do whatever is necessary to protect his knees and lower back. To stay in shape, I've worked with a physical therapist to develop a workout routine. It's divided into two separate parts, which I alternate in the gym spending roughly an hour each day. Each requires the use of some of the most common equipment found in gyms, including free weights. Regular visits to the gym help me maintain strength and flexibility, not to mention rearranging a bunch of the calories. They also make it much easier to handle the physical demands of the dance floor.

Speaking of calories, there is little that can be done when the food is too good. The food even at breakfast is wonderful. This, however, is when I get back to a meal with no fat, minimal carbohydrates, little sugar, and lots of fiber. Carefully picking several cereals and combining them with the fresh fruit that's available makes one good, healthy meal (by my standards) each day. This will make more sense to those who have seen what happens after six weeks of truly wonderful meals and desserts. The good news is that the prolonged periods of aerobic exercise hosts get dancing really do help burn off a lot of the carbohydrates, which would otherwise become a permanent part of their appearance.

Chapter 10 - APPEARANCE

As a host thinks and interacts like a classical gentleman of the world, he becomes aware of the value of looking the part. After all, he is a performer of sorts. The best often find that guests want to see and touch them as stars. Hence, they develop the ability to be well-groomed and well-dressed. This easy step sells the rest of the image even to the onlookers.

Ready For Another Evening

A host is expected to consistently be a more refined dresser than the majority of the guests. His daytime apparel is described as good country club or resort clothing. The best will comfortably set an elegant, not ostentatious or gaudy, look all the time. He, like any senior staff member on duty, would naturally shy away from T-shirts and tank tops, jeans, sloppy pants and/or shirts, and tennis shoes or sandals.

Given his self-dependent image, the best of the best will choose to dress smartly regardless of what the guests and other hosts might wear. One well-respected host of long standing always wears a jacket throughout the evening. On several of the elite ships, and on world cruises, refined translates to a jacket and tie even for *casual* night attire. On formal nights hosts don a tuxedo. The specifics about this wardrobe are in chapter 12.

Chapter 11 - ROMANCE AND AGENDAS

Romance is an exciting part of fantasies and life, yet the importance of side-stepping it in the real world of a host will be equally clear to the respected dream weaver. There undoubtedly will be women traveling with dreams of romance as part of their vacation. When a host becomes the focus of these dreams, it's flattering and stimulating. He'll let it charge his ego, but he stops right there since it can sail him into Titanic trouble. Romantic attraction is electrifying and can produce rewards far greater than a dancing vacation or cruise. However, it's destructive when one is hosting.

The most common aspect of the host's role emphasized throughout this book is assuring that unbiased attention is equitably given to all the unaccompanied ladies. As working hosts know, it's tough to achieve that balance, and the impression of it for the onlookers, even without adding the complexity of romantic involvement. Complicate the jealousies that come with a group of ladies competing for attention by adding the anxieties that accompany playing with forbidden fruit, and it will be obvious why more than one host has been relieved to be ejected from the ship. This side of the situation doesn't even open the pandora's box belonging to a cruise line or resort containing legal requirements to avoid problems related to sexual misconduct between its people and their guests. Ah heck, nobody will notice, right? It was her idea, right?

Experienced gentlemen know that no activity, romantic or otherwise, will go unnoticed. The role places hosts in one of the brightest spotlights all the time. There are a lot of eyes attracted to them. Too many of those eyes belong to envious, frustrated people, coupled or not.

Here's the personal side of the problem. It's not unusual for accusations of improper behavior against a host to be orchestrated by a third party, or later by the lady herself when she feels jealous or spurned. How are you going to keep that from happening while in the role of a host? Experienced hosts just don't risk a situation with a guest they've known less than ten days which could be construed improperly by anyone. History holds a number of cases where she/they deliberately turned against the man. Additionally, know that if she doesn't talk about it now, she will later!

This actually happened, believe it or not. Shortly after a significant cruise line invited me to help them improve their host program, I began dating a lovely professional woman. We met at a studio where I danced when in that part of the country. She'd gotten interested in learning to dance properly after a cruise some months earlier where she'd enjoyed dancing with the hosts. In the safety and honesty of our association, she told me of her relationship with one of those hosts while on the cruise. He was a man from a different part of the country with whom I'd shared a couple of cruises and dance floors a year earlier, learning then of his extra-curricular behavior. She and I both knew that she wasn't the first or the one and only for him. Not because of her or me, but because of his own emotional instability, he's no longer hosting.

Creating such a situation is unforgivable on the part of a host and not tolerated by any of the organizations. The rule is that there must never be a hint of romantic involvement attached to a host.

> *A host can expect that any romantic involvement while on an assignment will result in his being immediately and formally dismissed. If at sea, he'll be disembarked at the next port of call to find and pay for his own way home.*

Regardless of which agent or organization is providing the host, everyone understands that the program exists to motivate people to have a memorable vacation. That includes making new friends while participating openly in new or deeply treasured activities like dancing. When guests lose faith in a host for whatever reason, the whole program suffers.

Could there be other reasons for romantic endeavors? It's not uncommon for them to be the prelude to other agendas. I know of a lady who has used a group of cruisers over several years now to facilitate her locating the men she's married. She's subsequently divorced one after another continually improving her life style.

If you saw the movie *Out to Sea*, you saw both of these scenarios fully exposed. Do you remember the ending? Walter Matthau and

Jack Lemon left the ship in a hurry hoping not to be caught. They escaped before the end of the cruise in one of the ship's rescue boats. As only luck would have it, they came ashore where they happened to run into the ladies they had been pursuing during their cruise. That is a reasonable portrayal of how at least the romantic indiscretion is dealt with even today. That's not the way to begin a relationship or return home prematurely to ones friends. By the way, do you remember who had the money as *Out to Sea* ended?

A few gentlemen, over the years, have met women while hosting and later gotten married. Some of those couples have returned as guests and enjoyed recalling the events that brought them together. These were men who properly fulfilled their hosting role, and who then followed up and went on to develop their relationships later.

Think about these warnings, your agenda(s), and decide what you're going to do about these encounters now. It's too late after you're aboard the ship and swimming in an ocean with piranhas you can't get away from.

vanLee Hughey

IV. HOW TO GET INVOLVED IN HOSTING

Sound like the lifestyle for you? Are you ready to sail the oceans and visit the capitals of the world in exchange for dancing a bit? If your answer is yes, get busy and update your Passport. Make certain that its expiration date is more than a year away. Most agents and cruise lines will not accept them when they are closer to the expiration date. It takes time to get a passport, including the reissue of one that's approaching its expiration. That may prove to be time you don't have. Your first call may be for an assignment next week.

One Thursday afternoon, a man stopped into the office of a private organization that uses hosts for its cruising dance program to inquire about the company's application process. He was in town dancing at a local ballroom competition. The organization had a cruise leaving Sunday and had just come up a man short. Since he had the credentials, he was offered the opportunity. However, he didn't have his passport with him. After a few frantic telephone calls, he was able to have it overnighted to his hotel. He bought a few new clothes, arrived at the airport Sunday morning, and was on his way to the ship. They liked him and he stayed with them for years thereafter.

The next step is to start contacting agents who book hosts. The adventurous will contact the cruise companies directly. That's not how I recommend getting started to those attending the dance host certification seminar. Certified graduates learn more effective approaches, and to be wary of organizations advertising hosted dance cruises, and why. Their attraction to the ladies is the apparent low cost, which often means that you end up paying too much to be there in inferior conditions. Admittedly, there are exceptions, but it helps to know which is which.

There was a time when most cruise lines took their host programs seriously, recruiting their own gentlemen. Those times, like much of the elegance that used to be the hallmark of cruising, are all but gone. Today, most of the cruise industry relies on private agencies to provide gentlemen for their ships. Such agencies contract the man's services for a fee. That fee may or may not include various additional and unexpected charges. Stated simply, you're paying for the right to work. Not so hot, eh?

About now you might say, "Hey, what happened to providing the cruise in exchange for doing the work?" For the most part that disappeared when the cruise industry decided it was too costly to maintain the graciousness and elegance of cruising. Yet, the cost to you should be a fraction of that paid by the guests when you can get an invitation to be a host. My objective is to give you the information needed so you get invited back as often as you want by handling each assignment successfully.

Beyond the capability of this text, I help and recommend placement of men—whose qualifications I can certify—into the selection routine. This is done through said seminar. Once you're ready to have your dancing ability and social skills put to the test in a safe setting, checkout Appendix I. The process also facilitates your contact with the companies and agents best suited to your interests. While certification helps assure recruiters that they are enlisting men who are ready to properly represent them, it helps you get the most for your effort. One man just getting started did a one hundred-day cruise circling a good part of the globe this spring worth at least twenty thousand dollars.

In any event, begin by preparing a résumé detailing your dancing ability and have it endorsed by a competent ballroom instructor. Do not have them lie for you since you'll clearly be tested by the guests if by no one else. Last fall a likable gentleman talked his way into perhaps the finest cruise-based program there is. Within three evenings several of the ladies who are very understanding, but experienced dance cruisers had reported his incompetence to the cruise director and had called the company's home office to report the problem. The man was greatly relieved, I'm sure, when he was removed from the ship shortly thereafter. That's grief and expense you don't need to experience. He had to pay his own fare home.

Similarly, your social attributes should also be mentioned in that résumé. It's a good idea to include an accurate 8 x 10 full-length photo of yourself. I suggest it be in a good dance pose with an attractively dressed, older lady. With these in hand, prepare a short letter of introduction for the package.

With all of that said and the wealth of guidance distilled in this book, you have my best wishes for immediate and long-running success as a dance host! Appendix I provides information on the certification seminar should you be interested in my help getting started or improving your chances at getting selected as a cruise ship dance host.

vanLee Hughey

V. ASSIGNMENT GUIDELINES

The remainder of this book is a carefully structured guided tour through the issues facing you after saying yes to an invitation. Here are matters to be dealt with from the time you accept an assignment until returning home again.

vanLee Hughey

VI. PREPARATION

Have you just gotten a phone call from an agent offering you an assignment? Congratulations, you're about to step into a marvelous role. May you succeed and have the best time of your life. Whether this is your first or your fiftieth trip, the best way to achieve those payoffs is to have the answers to the issues discussed in the previous chapters.

Before committing to an assignment, make certain that your emotional and physical health, the state of your affairs at home, and so forth, are such that you can comfortably be gone. The rewards of each trip depend on your contentment with the assignment and ability to leave the real world behind. Only then is it possible to actively perform the host's magic as a socializer, a dancer, and a team player from the time you arrive at the resort or walk aboard the ship.

Once you have said yes, it's grossly unfair to everyone to cancel an established assignment unless it's truly necessary and there are several weeks for them to refill your slot.

vanLee Hughey

Chapter 12 - WARDROBE

The most unsettling issue requiring the best planning for almost every invitation is: what to wear. There are several required outfits that each host wears during every assignment. That part is easy. What he dresses like the rest of the time will depend entirely on his planning. Guidance from the agent, organization, or cruise line will not go beyond the standard outfits.

The guideline when choosing the wardrobe is to mix and match the clothes of a conservative gentleman. The intent will be to dress better than what might be suitable for the guests. The host is expected to set a dressy, not ostentatious or gaudy, tone all the time. His choice of clothing will yield the appearance of a well-bred gentleman in the classical sense.

Hosts are expected to bring all the clothes they need. I'm a bargain shopper, and have fun haggling over the price of things to enhance my wardrobe in little shops around the world. Many of the guests, primarily onlookers whom one may never meet, will notice any extreme. Hence, the emphasis on conservative. Part of looking good includes keeping things cleaned and pressed. Regardless of the cleaning procedure and discounts offered, remember that laundry services take time. Even pressing is not overnight, so it's necessary to plan ahead.

There are published dress codes for each evening of a cruise which should be listed in your cruise ticket or packet. There will normally be at least two formal nights. The rest will be either informal or casual. For a host, formal means a tuxedo, informal means a jacket worn with a tie, and casual means at least a long-sleeved, dressy shirt unless told otherwise. On several of the elite ships and on world cruises, a casual night often translates to a jacket and tie for the evening. There are also specific things to be worn for special events. We'll look at the attire for those events in chapter 27 when we talk about feature appearances and formal events. Typically, hosts must bring the following standard well-fitted clothing for evening wear and special functions.

The two standard outfits are:

1- **The Uniform:** hosts have universally included in their wardrobe a combination called the uniform: DARK BLUE BLAZER, WHITE SHIRT AND AN APPROPRIATE TIE, WHITE SLACKS, WHITE SOCKS, AND WHITE SHOES. Verify what that combination is for each assignment. It will be worn by all hosts for special events.

2. **Formal Attire:** hosts appear in a well-fitted black tuxedo consisting of: black slacks matching the jacket, a white tux shirt, a black bow tie, a black stud set and cufflinks, a black cummerbund, black socks and black formal shoes. The shoes are usually patent leather.

Host in Uniform

This formal combination will be worn on at least two occasions during each cruise. Each host will also need an equally formal white dinner jacket. This will be worn in place of the black tux jacket when there are more than two formal nights during a cruise.

3. **Other:** Beyond those specific outfits, each man will usually be left on his own. There have been hosts who wore only the uniform when not in their tuxedo. They normally have a great deal more latitude than that, as long as it looks equally good to the guests.

The left column in the adjacent table is a typical wardrobe for the evening activities of a ten to fourteen-day luxury-class cruise.

Guideline to Evening Wear:	**Four-month Wardrobe Expansion**
Navy blazer *(1)	
White slacks *(1)	(2 Instead of 1) May use pair from the Daytime Clothes
White shirts (2)	
Appropriate ties (2)	(3)
White socks (2)	(3)
White dress shoes *that you can dance in* (1)	
Sports coat (1), conservative*	(3)
Appropriate slacks* (1 blue)	(2 blue)
(1 black)	(2 black)
Appropriate non-white shirts (3)	(6)
Appropriate ties (2)	(6)
Dance shoes, Black (1)	(2)
Black Tuxedo complete* (1)	
Tuxedo shirts with French cuffs (2), no ruffles	
Studs and cufflink set (1)	(2 sets)
Bow ties (1), not the collar clip-on type	(2 tieable)
Cummerbund (1)	(2)
Black formal (patent leather) dress shoe (1)	
These must be comfortable to dance in for at least one hour.	
White Formal Dinner Jacket* (1)	
Elegant long-sleeved, dressy (2) shirts*	(4)
that you can dance in	

* I suggest a tropical weight that breathes - consider cotton/lycra blends.

As the length of the cruise increases, adding another pair of slacks, a shirt, and sports coat can create several combinations for variety. The right column shows the additions made for a world cruise. That cruise was made up of four individual 25-day segments. Since navy blue, black, and white are part of the required evening-wear, adding sports coats of different colors can alter one's appearance nicely. The required white slacks usually work well with whatever sports coats I carry. This almost doubles the number of outfits possible with a single jacket. By carefully mixing and matching things as much as possible, you'll have the most outfits while carrying the fewest pieces possible. There is limited closet space, and that is cut in half when sharing the cabin with another host.

Shopping carefully, it's possible to find that there are several tuxedos and sports coats made from very light-weight fabrics which breathe well. The fabric is important because you'll be dancing in these clothes, often with a long-sleeved shirt, for several hours each night. The ballrooms are adequately ventilated, but they are normally air conditioned for the comfort of the majority of the guests in attendance. Most of these will be the lightly dressed ladies waiting to dance and onlookers, all sipping on something cold. The host, however, is exercising in a coat and tie.

Daytime Wear:

What a host looks like during the day is almost as important as at night, but much less definite. His daytime clothing has been described as country club or resort casual. That translates to collared shirts, polo shirts, casual slacks with loafers or deck shoes. Shorts and clean tennis shoes are limited to visits to the gym, playing basketball or paddle tennis. When on a ship, "whites" during the day (slacks, socks and shoes with a solid-colored shirt) make a good showing. Uniformity of appearance for the hosts during the daytime is not expected.

Guideline to Daytime Clothes: **Four-month Wardrobe Expansion**

Black slacks (1)
   Coordinated patterned short sleeved shirts (4)
   Solid short-sleeved shirts (1)
   Coordinated patterned long-sleeved shirts (1)   (2 instead of 1) May use an evening casual shirt.

   Black casual shoes (1)
Blue slacks (1)
   Coordinated patterned short-sleeved shirts (2)
   Coordinated patterned long-sleeved shirts (1)   (2) May use an evening casual shirt

   Off-white slacks (1)
   Wear with black and blue coordinated shirts
   Off-white casual shoes (2): 1 deck shoes, 1dressier
Khaki safari slacks (1) for escorting tours
   Blue short-sleeved shirt
   Off-white long-sleeved shirt
   Safari vest
Sweater or all purpose jacket (1)
Cap (1)

T-shirts and tank tops are not acceptable wear for a host, nor are jeans, sloppy pants or shirts, or sandals. Be sure to pack a swimsuit, possibly snorkeling supplies, exercise clothes for the gym, and an umbrella.

Chapter 13 - FINANCIAL PLANNING

Are you really ready to be away from home? It was midyear several years ago, and I was soaking up the Mediterranean sun, cruising as a host to a private group on perhaps the nicest of the luxury ships at sea. We were a week into a twelve-day cruise. During one of the bands breaks, I got caught up in a conversation with the cruise director. I'd sailed with him before and respected him immensely, knowing that he was recognized across the industry as one of the best in the business. So, I was flattered when he asked if I would remain on the ship when my group disembarked in Athens. With a couple of adjustments to my schedule at home which I was able to make using the guest's e-mail system, I was able to accept his invitation. When I asked how long would he like me to stay, his reply was, "As long as you like." Now, that threw me. I remained on board for roughly four more weeks, but then had to return home to pay the mortgage, utilities, and several other recurring bills.

Since that experience, I've arranged for all my bills and credit cards to be paid electronically. The only two recurring expenses that I've not been able to automate the payment for are my annual automobile tags and one credit card. I'm now able to manage that card account using the Internet. With the ability to extend the due date for filing tax returns, I'm able to do cruises year round without any concerns about my financial responsibilities. A whole lot of planning and a bit of testing in this area will provide flexibility and untold peace of mind while hosting.

The better prepared one is for being away from home, the more able he will be to capitalize on the opportunities that present themselves. This means minimizing land-based responsibilities and assuring that bills are paid automatically.

Chapter 14 - PERSONAL EXPENSES

What about cash to carry when leaving home? This depends on a person's interests and shopping habits, but $50 in cash for each port day is a good starting point. Gift and souvenir buyers may need more cash, as well as extra luggage space. I'm not a big souvenir collector and have gotten away from the need to buy something at each stop, so $50 cash per week is adequate.

The best approach for adjusting the basic amount of money to be carried begins by looking at the length of the assignment and its itinerary. Any specific things you'll want to do should stand out and will help determine how much money you may spend. For those planning to take a side trip (excursion) to the Taj Mahal, for example, there will be things they'll want to buy. Hence, they'll put more cash in their pocket before leaving home. Excursions and off-ship meanderings will almost always involve out-of-pocket expenses.

The farther one travels away from the United States, the more necessary it will be to purchase foreign (local) currency. For example, when visiting Scandinavia, Europe, Asia, Africa and South America. Logical isn't it? How many of the stores that you shop in at home accept the euro or yen? When going ashore in distant places postcards, trinkets, gifts, taxi fares, beverages, and the like will require the local currency. Credit cards won't work for many of these things, including internet connectivity.

For most purchases, from the little ones just mentioned to those involving significant amounts of money, you'll do better using the local currency. Watch what happens when they work up a price in U.S. dollars. A cyber café recently charged 600 of their local currency for an hour of internet connection. They would accept US$3 for a half hour or US$5 for an hour. The exchange rate was roughly 200 to US$1. Hence, it would have cost about double the local price to use American currency. Always ask what the internet use fee is and whether it's a modem (slow) or a broadband (high speed) connection. A small island in the Pacific wanted US$12 a half-hour on a modem connection and using a French keyboard. Ouch! For your information, the "period" on that keyboard is a <shift><comma> when you find it.

You may be able to buy the local currencies for the trip from your bank at home. By purchasing all the various currencies for a trip at one time before departure, you'll pay only one commission on the large transaction. If each currency is bought separately along the way, there will be at least the same commission rate charged on every small transaction. I typically buy US$10 to $20 of the currencies I expect to use and carry it with me when ashore in that country. Thus, I have some of the local currency with me even on Sundays and on those occasions when there are no money exchanges around.

Transition of the twelve eurozone (European) countries to the standard euro currency effective January 1, 2002, simplified and reduced the number of currencies needed when visiting Europe. The twelve countries are Austria, Belgium, Finland, France, Germany, Greece, Ireland, Italy, Luxembourg, the Netherlands, Portugal and Spain. In the foreseeable future, mini-states like the Vatican, San Marino, and Monaco may also join the European Monetary Union (EMU). Having traveled much of the world, I've enjoyed learning the history that has led mankind to where we are. Having crossed the borders into all of these countries over the years, I've changed the currency in my wallet at the same time. I'm interested to see if these historically discordant areas are able to work together with a common currency. Perhaps you'll be hosting there too in the next few years to experience how history unfolds.

The exception to using the local currency rule is when you know the exchange rate at the time, and can negotiate a better deal in dollars, then, charge it to your Visa[7], MasterCard[7] or American Express[7]. These are the only ones that are universally accepted worldwide. Occasionally, even one or another of these may not be accepted. It's a good idea to have at least two if not all three of these to assure that you'll be able to charge transactions when you wish. I was in Greece and wanted to charge a negotiated US$28 purchase. The vendor accepted my credit card, but for whatever reason, she couldn't make the electronic connection for approval. I had negotiated a good deal that I didn't want to lose, but I didn't have the time to spend waiting for a telephone connection to that company. So I had the shop use one of the other cards, which processed straight through.

You'll also run up charges aboard the ship, but nothing that will require cash. Everything on the ship will be charged to your personal account. That account must be settled in full at the end of your assignment. It may be settled with cash, check or traveler's checks, as well as a major credit card. Credit card settlement is by far the fastest and most foolproof way to pay this account. It all happens automatically once the folks at the reception desk have made the necessary imprint of the credit card.

While in transit to or from an assignment, it's a good habit to have lots of US one and five-dollar bills in your pockets. When flying internationally, carry some of the local currency (s) for use in the airport(s) when changing planes en route to your destination.

Chapter 15 - PERSONAL MAINTENANCE ITEMS

Experienced travelers learn to take the toiletries that they'll need with them. Especially, those brand-specific items they're attached to. Things that would be common at home may not be available when out to sea. One may be able to buy things he's familiar with at a market when in port; then again, he may not. A couple of years ago, a Consumer Reports magazine published an article on a good combination insect repellant and sunblock. Having worn the OFF Skintastic[7] (with no DEET odor) from safari in Africa to the beaches in Polynesia, it is one of those brand specific items that go with me. Having had trouble finding it at home, I maintain a year's supply. Outside the U.S., no one knows what that product is. I've paid $20 on a ship for a 4.5 ounce tube of good 30 sunblock, but the mosquitoes loved it.

You may get lucky and discover that you like some of the things sold in the ship's shops. I was once asked to extend my cruise time by a month and ran out of hair spray. The ship didn't stock what I used. The nationally advertised brand available on board proved to be better and longer lasting, making it less expensive than the one I'd been buying at home.

Do you travel with an electric shaver or a digital camera battery charger? The luxury ships have provided a standard 110v 60 cycle as well as a separate 220v 50 cycle electrical outlet in each cabin since the early 1990s. However, even the nicest hotels and resorts outside of North America have not. Since that time, ships and most resorts have also provided at least a permanently mounted hair dryer in each cabin. If you prefer to use your own hair dryer or other lightweight electrical appliance, it will work fine on a ship. Electric irons are not permitted in ship cabins as they pose a serious fire hazard. Some of the best ocean liners provide a guest laundry with irons and ironing boards. A standard item in my suitcase is a compact, a three-outlet electrical **octopus**, and a handheld clothes steamer. There is typically only one 110v electrical outlet in a ship's cabin. It's at the desk. The octopus permits a couple of simultaneous connections.

If you're going to stay on land outside the United States, for example, before or after an assignment, remember that the rest of the world uses a 220v 50 cycle electrical system. Both the voltage and the wall plugs for connecting to it are totally different from the electrical system which is standard in the US. Hence, your 110v hair dryer will be fried without a power converter, if you manage to plug it in. The solution is to carry a complete 220v power converter kit that includes several different adapters. The adapters are critical because, even though most countries use the same 220v standard, many use totally different styles of wall plugs to connect to the power source.

By the way, batteries that are standard in the US may not be available on the ship or at a foreign resort. When available, they'll be expensive.

Chapter 16 - MEDICINES AND MEDICAL FACILITIES

As you plan for any assignment, be sure that you're in the physical and emotional health to handle the demands of the time away from home. A recent physical, eye exam, and dental checkup are more important than worrying about vitamins, simple medications, and toothpaste. It's to your advantage to be certain that nothing which can be caught by these examinations surprises you when the closest help could be two days away in Bora Bora.

Resorts do not tend to have on-site medical facilities. They do have a working relationship with a good, near-by clinic. Should the need for attention arise, the concierge can arrange for transportation there, or even an on-site visit by one of that country's doctors.

Cruise ships maintain a medical office staffed by nurses and at least one doctor, often licensed in a Scandinavian country, the United Kingdom, or Canada, though rarely in the US. These people are hired from their established practices to spend a block of time on the ship. The few visits I've made have left me feeling that I was in good hands. My impression is that the charges for an office visit are a bit high. These offices carry a wide array of medications, but obviously in limited quantities.

There is not a pharmacy on-board. Last year I became acquainted with an architect from Saudi Arabia who was cruising with his wife. Mid-way, he discovered that he had not packed enough insulin for the time he was booked. The medical office had something that would meet his medical needs until we reached the next port in Africa. The medical team helped him locate a facility there where he was able to get the specific insulin he needed.

When an ailment is more severe than the clinic can treat, the person will be transferred to a medical facility that can handle it at the next port.

Assuming they can give the person adequate treatment and get them transferred home, the traveler needs to have appropriate insurance.

It's good financial medicine to call your own provider before leaving home to be sure you're covered for any needed medical treatment onboard a ship or in a foreign country. I understand that many policies, including Medicare, pay nothing. My health insurer has honored the written statement for services rendered aboard ship, but not always without question. Recently, a fellow host introduced me to a Multi-Trip[7] policy from Travelex Insurance Services. That program is provided for those people doing a lot of this type of traveling. It's only good when the insured is more than fifty miles from home. It's less expensive than similar policies, and appears to provide more complete coverage both on board ship and in foreign countries. The good news is that I haven't had a reason to find out how well they deliver their coverage.

Given the best of health, it's wise to carry extra vitamin C, zinc, odorless garlic, and/or whatever you use to stimulate your immune system and medicate colds, or any other ailments, that may bother you. Anti-inflammatories like ibuprofen as well as aspirin, antihistamines, headache medication are also part of my supply list. These may be available in the resort's or ship's variety shop, but you'll pay dearly for them. Anything more specialized than vitamin C may be difficult to find when you're cruising the world. If you like and use breath mints, bring your choice along with you. Having these to share with the ladies and others is also a thoughtful touch.

Chapter 17 - DOCUMENTS

> CARRY A VALID PASSPORT with at least <u>six unused pages</u> in it
>
> WITH YOU ON EVERY ASSIGNMENT!

Passport: A valid passport carries an expiration date that is more than a year away. The reference to the unused pages in the passport is important because when traveling a lot, it can run out of space needed for visas and by Immigration Officials to enter their authorization stamp. In addition to a passport, there are various countries which require a visa for entry.

Visas: Normally when a visa is needed, the booking agent will notify you of that fact in advance. Always ask the booking agent about the need for a visa before going to the trouble and expense of getting one.

First, determine if you'll really need one. For example, for personal entry into St. Petersburg, Russia, you'll need a visa. However, if you're not going to leave the ship, or doing so only with a packaged shore excursion sponsored by the ship and you remain with that group, then you may not need to spend the $150 for a personal entry visa. On the other hand, for the ship to enter India, each passenger has to have his/her own personal visa. Recently, I was on a ship with a stop scheduled in southeast Asia. All the passengers were required to hand in their passport with the visa for that stop when initially boarding the ship.

Second, determine if you're going to be reimbursed for the cost of the visa. It's worth several hundred dollars of your money to know the answers about visas before accepting an assignment on a ship.

The booking agent may provide a mail-in source for your visa. I've found dealing with a local visa service or ordering it myself has been faster and less expensive. The service has been able to take the needed photos right there on the spot. When you go to get a visa, remember to take your passport with you! You'll have to surrender it to them. They'll submit it with the application and then return it to you with the visa inserted. This process takes at least a week, so make sure you have enough time and get it done as early as possible.

Other: A good practice is to photocopy your drivers' license, the photo/issuance page of your passport, and your birth certificate. Carry these, along with a current unused passport photo, in a totally separate place from your travel documents. Should your passport be lost or stolen, these copies will help get a new one issued by an American Embassy while you're out of the country.

Chapter 18 - PACKING IT ALL IN

Do you spend too much time and frustration packing? Have you ever been several days into a trip and a thousand miles from home or land when you discovered something you really needed had not been packed? Early in my hosting days while cruising the Eastern Caribbean with a private group, I discovered that my white belts had not been packed. Shops rarely carry white belts, so I ended up without. Here's a simple pre-packing process I've developed to reduce the time and errors, and eliminate the frustration.

Packing is simplified by using two forms that help get everything laid out quickly. The forms are completed before and modified as I'm laying out my belongings.

CLOTHING FORM, shows in detail the number of evening outfits and combinations being carried and why. It helps limit the items carried to a minimum while getting the greatest variety from the combinations. Tuxes aside, if I can't get at least two outfits out of one jacket, without adding slacks or shirts, then I don't carry that jacket. Perfecting the entries on the upper half of the form has proven to be an effective way to thin down the number of pieces to what will actually be used during an assignment.

This form is perfected while I'm pulling and checking out the clothes for the assignment from the drawer or closet. Should an item be found unsuitable for this trip, it's easy to replace it with another and update the form. When doing a private dance group, I'll often wear a tail coat, replacing the tux jacket, for the first Formal night. It may be worn again by changing the shirt style and neckwear significantly, and perhaps even the slacks, for the last formal evening. When hosting for a resort or cruise line, I leave the tails at home, putting the classical black tux jacket back on the form. The bottom half of the form, the inventory portion, helps me eliminate duplicates and verify that all the things needed have been pulled.

Clothing Caribbean – Zenith
December 30 – January 6, 20xx

	Jacket	*Slacks*	*Shirts*	*Neck Piece*	*Shu-Soc-Blt*	*Accsry*
Tux:	Blk Sprkl	Blk Tux Sprkl	Wht Tux w-Red Line	Blk Bow	Blk-Blk	Blk Studs CB-Blk
	Blk RhnStn Trim	•	Blk Prtn Frnt	RhnStn	Blk-Blk	CB-Blk
Informal:	Shrt Blu	Ivory	OffWht (ss)	Blu-Gld Lions	Wht-Wht-Wht	
	•	DrkBlu	DrkBlu	Wht-Blu End	Blk-Blk-Blk	
	Peach	Ivory	OffWht (ss)	Hawaiin Strng	Wht-Wht-Wht	
	•	✦	Blk-Gld Inly	Ephnt BCvr	Wht-Blk-Blk	
	•	DrkBlu	Lite Blu	Elton Blu	Blk-Blk-Blk	
Causal:		Blk Dance	Mexican Formal	Gld Choker w-RhnStne	Blk-Blk-Mexican	
		DrkBlu	Med Euro	Gold Rose	Blk-Blk-Titanic	
		Blk Dance	White Crmpl	RhnStn	Blk-Blk-Blk	
Transit:	Blk Lthr Like	Blk Lthr Like	White Crumple		Blk-Blk-Blk	

Casual - Informal Clothes Inventory

Slacks:			*Belts:*	
	Black	- Angel		Blk, Titanic
	Blue Drk	- Dress		Blk, Medium
	Ivory	- Dress		Wht, Medium
	Black	- Leather Like		

Shirts:	LONG SLEEVE - IN-FORMAL		*Shoes*	
	Blu	- Dark Dress		Blk, Patent
	Blu	- Euro		Blk, Dance
	Mexciab	- Formal		Blk, Dress Boot
	White	- Crumpled		OffWht - Dance
	Blk	- Gold Inlay		Ice, Docksider

SHORT SLEEVE - CASUAL

Black	- Forest	Blue	- Spotted	Orange	- Mexican
Black	- Leopard	Blue	- Island	OffWht	- 1
		Blue	- Lite		

Jacket: Black Leather Like

CLOTHING FORM

TRAVEL	SUPPLIES	
Toiletries:	**Personal Supplies:**	**Misc:**
Battery Shaver	Bedroom Slippers	32 Diskettes
Beard Shaver	Books to Read	Auto Bridge
Deodorant	Contacts	Calendar
Hair Brush &Comb	Eye Glasses	Camera& Tripod
Hair Barrettes	Exercise Outfit	Cassette Tapes
Hair Coloring	Swim Suit	Cereal Mix
Hair Spray	Foreign Monies	Crystal Bag
Hair Volumizer	Hat, Cap Type	Dance Shoe Brush
Hand Lotion	Jacket	Dictionary
Perfume	Shoe Spoon	Electrical Octopus
Shampoo / Rinse	Sunglasses	Exercise Log
Shaver	Sweater	Extension Cords
Sunscreen	Tennis Shoes	Protein Powder
Toothbrush	Tool Kit	Small Notebook
	Watch(es)	Travel Alarm
		White Shoe Clnr
Medications:	**Dance Supplies:**	**Foreign Supplys:**
Vitamins	Speakers	220v Hair Dryer
Medicine Kit	CD Player	Power Converter
Vitamins	Power Supplies	
Ibuprofen (Motrin)	Dance CD's	

A - WARDROBE   B - BIG CASE   C - SML WARDROBE   CO - CARRY-ON

TRAVEL SUPPLIES FORM

The clothes go on a portable clothing rack until packing time. With the clothes pulled and the form completed, it's a fast process to verify that the appropriate accessories are laid out. Last-minute changes are easily made, and the wardrobe for the trip is ready to pack.

TRAVEL SUPPLIES FORM, is a comprehensive checklist of all of the toiletries and miscellaneous supplies that I may want to have with me. It's a checklist used for each assignment. When I'm teaching, then the Dance Supplies items are packed. When doing Alaska, I'm not concerned with the Foreign Monies item and line through it. Everything that will go is pulled, checked off the list and laid out separately from the clothing.

Using these forms helps assure that everything that will be needed is laid out in an organized fashion and in a short period of time. They then become my packing lists. Used while packing, they help assure that all the things are accounted for when the suitcases are closed. Since I record on the forms in which suitcase each of the items is packed, I have a detailed record of my property by suitcase should one ever be lost. Both of these forms are stored with my travel documents in my carry-on case. When working at the facility, the clothing form eliminates the quandary about what to wear each night or what goes with what.

Chapter 19 - LUGGAGE

Having determined the size of the wardrobe along with the personal supplies, after thinning them down at least once, it's a simple process to put everything in a couple of bags. Your thought at this point may be, do you have the right luggage to pack them in? That's not the place to begin.

Of primary importance is a carry-on case in which you can pack one complete uniform, traveling entertainment such as reading items, laptop computer, prescription medication, and the toiletries needed while en route. This starting place may seem a bit strange, but bear with me and you'll save yourself a lot of frustrations along the way.

The carry-on doesn't need to be a large case. Mine is probably half the size and weight of the case everyone else is lugging around. Proper packing of this one suitcase has taken the ravel out of travel for more than one host over the years. That's because once aboard the ship, it may be several hours before checked luggage is delivered to the room. This delivery delay may not provide the needed time to clean up and get properly groomed for the first evening's dance assignment and on-stage introductions. Hint: a lot of space can be saved if you'll wear the blue blazer of the uniform while traveling. Having all the things needed for this first night in hand when boarding the ship can be a lifesaver. The time can be used to learn the landscape or ship's layout, enjoy a nap, meet the other hosts, find out what the program is for the evening, etc., without concern about your razor, deodorant, and clothing.

Next, depending on how well you've reduced the size of your wardrobe, everything may fit in a medium-sized wheeled, wardrobe-type suitcase or two. It's best to pack the works in two medium-sized, wheeled cases that you can lift and carry. Besides avoiding overweight bag problems with the airlines, each of us is going to get exercise carrying our luggage every now and then. I carefully distribute the clothing for an assignment between the two cases. If one is delayed, I still have complete outfits in hand. Suggestion: don't fill any case more than two-thirds full. That will provide space in which to pack the treasures accumulated along the way for the trip home. Fill the extra space when starting the trip with bubble wrap or bags of packing peanuts, and discard that which isn't needed when returning home.

There are good reasons all the ships are selling at full price lots of suitcases and travel bags as each cruise comes to an end. With just a little forethought, you can avoid that expense. On long trips, like a 100-day World Cruise, I carry one large, wheeled case in which I nest and pack another medium-sized bag as if they were a single suitcase. That way I have an empty medium-sized bag with me for use on the way home if needed. This large case carries my bulkiest, and yet lightest, belongings.

Nested Suitcases - Plan Ahead

One last time, do yourself a favor by not stuffing your wardrobe and miscellaneous supplies into one or two suitcases making one of them 1) too heavy to handle, and 2) too full. If that happens, start over. Change something to spread and lighten the individual load. Do it in such a way that you will be able to lift and carry all the pieces. Once everything is packed well enough to survive all of the handling it will get, seal them up. There's one last essential thing to do—tag them.

   If you received a packet of materials (explained in chapters 20 and 21) including tickets from the cruise line, locate the baggage identification tags that are in there. Look for the cabin number on the cruise ticket. It may or may not yet have been assigned. Enter whatever is shown on the ticket legibly in the cabin number space provided, and your name, on the baggage identification tags. Attach one tag to each suitcase. I tape these tags to the side or top of the suitcase with wide, clear packaging tape to reduce the possibility of their getting torn off in transit. It's these tags, by cabin number or name when that's all you have, which will get the luggage delivered to your cabin.

VII. GETTING THERE

Working with a resort is usually a very simple process. Either you get yourself to their lobby or they send you the tickets needed to accomplish the same result. Just be sure that you and they agree on the method of transit they are having you use. The same two options exist when doing a ship, but the details which follow can be a great deal more complex.

vanLee Hughey

Chapter 20 - PERSONALLY ARRANGED TRANSIT

For those assignments when the cruise line is not providing the transportation, you'll have agreed to get yourself to the right dock on the right day and hour before the ship sets sail. In this scenario, it's possible that neither the agent nor the cruise line will send any documentation other than the agreement that you signed. You'll not receive the baggage identification tags mentioned in chapter 19 for labeling luggage. In this case, be especially certain that your personal identification tags are obvious on each suitcase.

In these circumstances, the cruise line will simply put your name on the ship's manifest, and give you your key at the ship. It's the booking agent's job to clarify all the details of this scenario with you including sailing date, boarding time, port location, recommended local lodging, who to contact in case of trouble and their 800 telephone numbers. Be sure to get these details in writing. Put these documents with your passport in the carry-on case. Ask the agent to mail these details, the normal passengers' information, and the shore excursion brochure(s) for the segments you're sailing.

Accepting an assignment where you're responsible for the transportation, means if your flight is delayed or canceled, neither the agent nor the cruise line will be of much assistance. However, do contact the agent immediately should that happen.

Since unpredictable flight delays do occur, it's wise to spend the night before embarking the ship in a hotel relatively near the dock, or with reliable transportation to it. Determine where the embarkation port is prior to making your lodging reservations. Know how you'll get from the hotel to the pier on the day of the week you board the vessel. The booking agent or the hotel should be able to give you that information when booking a room. If they can't, I'd suggest finding another hotel. Spending several dollars more for lodging, but knowing the answer to the transportation question, can save you a bundle.

Several years ago, I was vacationing in Portugal prior to sailing from Rome, Italy. Having been to Rome with various groups several times before, I decided to fly in and pick up the ship there for an assignment in the Mediterranean. Since I knew that "I knew" what I was doing, using a travel agency, I made affordable lodging arrangements downtown to do the tourist bit the day before. That meant taking a US$75 limo from the airport to the hotel the afternoon of my arrival. When at the hotel, I asked the driver if he could take me to the port to catch the ship in the morning. He was confused. He didn't understand what I was talking about because, 1) his English was only marginally better than my nonexistent Italian, and 2) there is no "port" in Rome. After figuring out what I was asking, he priced the trip at US$150. It would take over an hour and a half to reach Civitavecchia, which is the seaside port community serving Rome. This community is in the opposite direction from the one I'd taken from the airport. Staying in Rome doubled my distance from the port.

That's not all. I was shocked to learn that taxis weren't permitted to carry passengers beyond the city limits, and certainly not to Civitavecchia. Luckily, I'd ridden downtown in a limo rather than a taxi, the driver was licensed to leave the city and luckily he did appear right on schedule in the morning.

The moral of the story: validate your local lodging and transportation plans with travel people before booking, and carry lots of local money. Then, you can have a carefree, affordable time touristering without concern about missing the ship. Next time I pick up the ship in Rome, I'll go directly to and stay in a nice hotel in Civitavecchia. Then, I can take the train into Rome, if it's running. It will take me almost directly to the sights I want to visit for less than US$20 round trip. What I save in transportation costs will pay for both lodging and meals. Do factor these types of errors into the amount of money you carry. The limo driver didn't take credit cards or anything but Italian lire.

Chapter 21 - AGENT ARRANGED TRANSIT

Life is easier when the cruise line provides the air tickets and handles all of your bookings. They know where the ports are. They can book overnight lodging for you. They can arrange your transportation to the ship. If your flight is delayed, causing you to miss the ship's departure, the cruise line will normally work with the air carrier to arrange for you to reach the ship at its next port of call, which is usually the third day of the cruise.

The cruise line will mail travel documents, including baggage identification tags, to you close to the departure date. Immediately upon receipt, check everything carefully! Are the flights, cabin, cruise date and length correct and in accordance with your understanding of the assignment? Are the airline, dates, departure and return cities, etc., correct? Two weeks ago I received the materials for a five week cruise from Los Angeles to Amsterdam. They flew me from my home in Atlanta to Los Angeles properly, but booked my return from Amsterdam direct to Los Angeles. Not good when I'm expecting to be returned home. Check the materials you receive carefully immediately upon receipt and, if they don't agree with your understanding, call the agent without delay. It's way too late and the wrong place to discover the problem - at the airlines ticket counter in Amsterdam - the date of the flight.

In some cases, when the cruise line is providing the air transportation, the return flight home may be booked after you're at sea. Should that be the case, or should a change have to be made to your return reservations once out to sea, work with the ship's concierge and, again, carefully review whatever you receive. Do not assume that the tickets will just appear or that they will be correct.

Remember that piece of carry-on luggage? That's the place to carry your passport along with your airline tickets, the ship's ticket, itinerary that lists all the ports of call, and the list of the ship's agent's information at each port. These documents are in the packet from the cruise line. In them is the cruise line's 800 telephone number for you to call should you miss the ship.

Chapter 22 - IN TRANSIT

It's a good practice to have lots of U.S. one- and five-dollar bills as you leave home. I carry $20 in ones and $30 in fives distributed in various pockets as well as in my wallet. What isn't used traveling, will be once we are sailing. When flying internationally, pocket some of their local currency for use in the airports when changing planes and at the destination city. No sense in being locked out of the men's room or unable to buy a newspaper or cup of coffee during a two-hour layover in London while connecting to Copenhagen because you packed their currency in a suitcase.

Be aware that while flying to meet the ship, you may be on a flight with cruise passengers. It pays to behave graciously like a host even then. Dress well and function with the same social graces as if on duty. At the same time, be sensitive to the airline staff. Those onlookers who will haunt you on the ship may be doing just that while you're in transit with them. First impressions do stick.

While waiting for a connecting flight from Paris to Venice, I watched a fairly handsome, well-dressed American nervously bothering the various gate agents about some things. He was loud enough to draw attention to whatever he was asking. Neither his tone of voice nor manner of interaction was pleasant. I watched him rather abruptly board the flight ahead of me. Imagine my surprise to be introduced to him in Venice as the other host boarding the ship. His manners were only slightly masked throughout the assignment. No surprise, this was his internal reference to the world. Remember the discussion about attitude in the section on characteristics and expectations?

To the airline, you or I are just another one of their bargain-basement passengers when the cruise line provides the ticket. This didn't sit well with our friend. Cruise line staff and hosts travel at the lowest contractible fares. The bottom line is that we're just regular passengers vying for seating and attention like everyone else.

VIII. ON BOARD AS A HOST

Wow. Here you are anywhere from a few hundred miles from home to half-way around the world. The adventure is about to begin. Sometimes even a familiar adventure can be more fulfilling if you have a decent map of the territory. I hope you'll find the following to be just that.

Ships' Lobby

85

vanLee Hughey

Chapter 23 - ARRIVAL

At the finest resorts, arrival will be like that at any good hotel. Catching a ship, however, is a totally different experience.

The departure city where a cruise begins is almost always the end of the previous cruise for a shipload of people. They normally begin disembarking the ship around 9 am. Obviously, it'll be several hours before the crew can get rid of all that luggage, finish replacing all the linen and supplies in the cabins, and otherwise prepare the just vacated ship to welcome a whole new load of incoming guests aboard.

Guests arriving in town the morning of departure are often taken to a hotel with a well-stocked courtesy suite. Sometimes they're treated to a tour of the city. Such a tour is a nice way to see some of the sights, in Honolulu for example. These would be missed if the people were sidetracked to a hotel or taken directly to the ship.

The downside is that everyone is probably tired and anxious to be aboard. That's a natural reaction, but not necessarily doable for the ship. When you're one of those tourists, the ability to be a positive influence during this time can be very valuable. Pleasant words and smiles can work wonders. Tip: If you're in control of your arrival time at the ship, avoid frustrating delays by arriving a half hour or more after the ship starts its boarding process.

By mid-afternoon, busloads of guests will be arriving at the pier so they can board the ship. Along with the guests, you'll check in at the reception desk either before entering the ship or onboard. If you've gotten yourself to the ship with the understanding that your name would be on the manifest, simply check in like everyone else. Tell the clerk who you are and what is going on. Have a copy of the assignment agreement and any other supporting paperwork with you. You will receive cabin information along with keys and any baggage tags needed for your luggage.

Once aboard the ship and in your cabin, relax and perhaps change shirts. Study the deck plan, which should be with the stationery package in your cabin. Then, enjoy a walk through the vessel. Introduce yourself at the reception (front) desk and ask about a name tag for the assignment. Locate the lounges where there will be dancing and learn what they're called. Check out both the show and movie theaters, coffee shops, dining room(s), lido restaurant, etc. Say hello to some of your fellow travelers as you make the rounds. Take the initiative and say "hi" even though it won't feel like you're a host yet.

Checked luggage becomes the next issue for everyone. That luggage will have reached the ship in several different ways. At the airport, it may be loaded and transported separately from its owners or unloaded from their bus and claimed by them at the pier only to be taken away for bulk transfer aboard the ship. Eventually, it's delivered to the owners stateroom by the ship's crew. This will be several hours after its owner is in the cabin.

Arrival - Where's My Luggage

The delay is caused by the number of suitcases being schlepped around the ship. Though effective at delivering the luggage, the staff may be handling several *thousand* bags. It just takes time. Multiply the number of bags you checked by the number of people boarding the ship. That total may be low. I know two delightful ladies who cruise together and who arrive with at least twenty checked suitcases. The cabin number on the baggage identification tag that we discussed previously is the key to this process. Being aware of the process and what's going on will be helpful as you notice the impatience of the guests. Later when we talk about handling complaints it'll make sense why you simply send the "missing luggage people" to the front desk.

In recognition of these delays, the first evening's dress is usually Casual. Some of the early seating guests may only have the clothes they traveled in available by their dinner time. If you are part of the evening's introductions made at the Welcome Aboard show(s), or aren't told what your apparel should be, play safe and dress in the uniform.

The value of a properly packed carry-on bag can't be stressed enough. With a fresh casual shirt in your carry-on luggage that goes with your travel slacks, you'll be able to look sharp between arrival and dinner. In the best scenario, your arrival at the ship, with luggage in hand, precedes that of the passengers. Personally carrying your luggage aboard eliminates these frustrating delays. This is one of those beneficial exercise times that we talked about in the luggage chapter.

Chapter 24 - GETTING STARTED - DAILY PROGRAM

Waiting in the cabin when you first arrive should be a name tag and two important documents.

The cruise ship will make the name tag. Wear it whenever you're out and about the ship. If it's not in the cabin, ask about it at the reception desk. If it becomes broken or lost, have one of the clerks at the reception desk get it replaced as soon as possible.

Next, there should be a card indicating which dinner seating, and in which dining room when there is more than one, you're assigned to. Typically, there are two dinner seatings—early, around 6:15 pm, and main (late), around 8:30 pm. If this card/information is missing, ask the host you're rooming with, one of the other experienced hosts, the dance instructors, or the Maitre d'Hotel to which seating you've been assigned.

Finally, there should be the program of this day's activities. This is the guide to everything going on around the ship by time and place. Learn the program's layout and content since it will be the guide to when and where you're working. If there are dance instructors onboard for the cruise, they'll often be responsible for the hosts and the dance program. They'll be the ones to answer your questions. The staff at the reception desk can tell you if there are resident dance instructors onboard. You can always get a copy of the daily program at the reception desk in the lobby.

Immediately study this first daily program to determine 1) when the mandatory lifeboat drill will be held, 2) when the evening's welcome aboard show(s) will begin in relation to the dinner seatings (early or late), and 3) when, as well as where, the evening dancing will take place. Look to see if there is scheduled dancing before dinner in addition to the regular evening dancing. Are you part of the welcome aboard introductions? Ask one of the team members mentioned above if the hosts will be introduced during these welcome aboard shows. Assume that your dress for the evening will be the uniform, but do ask.

While checking out these issues with the other hosts or dance instructors, confirm who is eating at which seating, and the time(s) you're dancing. This liaison is part of the teamwork that assures that the hosts are in the right place at the right time and are working together. As the cruise progresses, times and places may change with no indication other than in the Daily Program. One or another of the hosts may not see a scheduled event. Prevent these problems by communicating with each other.

vanLee Hughey

Welcome Aboard

GOOD AFTERNOON

2:00pm	**Embarkation for all our guests. Welcome Aboard.** Captain Egil Giske, Commander, along with Hotel Director Per Nilsen, Cruise Director Paul McFarland, the officers, staff, and crew of Crystal Harmony, welcome you aboard for this "Majestic Glaciers" cruise.

2:00pm – 7:00pm	**Salon Appointments.** Stop by to make your hair and beauty appointments. *(Bridge Lounge today only).*	Bridge Lounge	6
2:00pm – 6:00pm	**Spa and Gym Tours** are available with Greg Steer, your Fitness Director. Ask Greg about personal training, Body Composition Analysis, and a free consultation.	Crystal Spa	12
3:30pm – 4:30pm	**Crystal Afternoon Tea Time.** Enjoy tea and pastries.	Palm Court	11

4:00pm	**All guests back on board please.**
4:15pm	**Mandatory Lifeboat Muster.** All guests who embarked in San Francisco are required to attend this drill. Please listen to the ship's P.A. for further instructions.
4:45pm	**Crystal Harmony sets sail for Alaska.**

5:00pm – 6:00pm	**Champagne Sail Away.** Enjoy complimentary Champagne as we sail under the picturesque Golden Gate Bridge and "North to Alaska!"	Lido Deck	11

ITINERARY
SAN FRANCISCO, CALIFORNIA TO SAN FRANCISCO, CALIFORNIA

Date	Port	Port Times	Dress Code	Galaxy Lounge Show	Crystal Dining Room Dinner	Movie in the Hollywood Theatre
August 13	San Francisco	Depart: 4:45pm	Casual	Welcome Show	Bon Voyage Dinner	*Someone Like You*
August 14	At Sea	Cruising	Formal	*Cole!*	Captain's Welcome Dinner	*Miss Congeniality*
August 15	At Sea	Cruising	Informal	Classical Concert	Dinner	*Head Over Heels*
August 16	Ketchikan	8:30am – 2:30pm	Casual/'50s	*Rock Around the Clock*	'50s Dinner	*Heartbreakers*
August 17	Skagway	10:00am – 6:00pm	Casual	Cabaret Showtime	*Guest Chef Dinner	*Enemy at The Gates*
August 18	Hubbard Glacier	1:00pm – 2:30pm	Formal	*Million Dollar Musicals*	French Dinner	*Spy Kids*
August 19	Juneau	7:00am – 5:00pm	Informal	Classical Concert	Neptune Dinner	*The Mexican*
August 20	Sitka	7:00am – 2:00pm	Informal/ Medieval	*Excalibur!*	Royal Feast Dinner	*The Wedding Planner*
August 21	At Sea	Inside Passage	Informal	Variety Showtime	Dinner	*The Amati Girls*
August 22	Vancouver	9:00am – Midnight	Casual	Cabaret Showtime	*California Dinner	*The Dish*
August 23	Victoria	7:00am – 1:00pm	Formal	*Spirit of America*	Captain's Farewell Dinner	*See Spot Run*
August 24	At Sea	Cruising	Casual	Farewell Show	Dinner	*Down to Earth*
August 25	San Francisco	Arrive: 6:45am	D I S E M B A R K A T I O N			

Itinerary, times, and shows are subject to change.   *Also *Casual Dining* at the Trident Grill

Crystal Harmony • Monday, August 13, 2001

Example - Daily Program Front

92

Evening Entertainment

GOOD EVENING

Time	Event	Venue	
5:30pm – 6:30pm & 7:45pm – 8:30pm	**Tom Daniels** plays the Crystal Piano as you relax and enjoy a pre-dinner cocktail.	Crystal Cove	5
5:30pm – 6:15pm & 7:45pm – 8:30pm	**Dance** to the music of the Manila Diamonds. Join your Ambassador Hosts.	Palm Court	11
5:45pm – 6:30pm & 7:45pm – 8:30pm	**Charlie Shaffer** entertains at the piano bar. Enjoy this fine entertainer as he performs a variety of music in the...	Avenue Saloon	6
7:00pm – 8:45pm	**Salon Appointments.** Stop by to make your hair and beauty appointments. *(Crystal Plaza desk, this evening only).*	Crystal Plaza	5
8:30pm & 10:30pm	**Movie:** *Someone Like You.* Ashley Judd stars as a young woman who begins an extensive study of the male animal and becomes a sex columnist. PG-13; 1:37.	Hollywood Theatre	6
9:30pm – 12:30am	**Charlie Shaffer** sings and entertains at the piano bar – a great time!	Avenue Saloon	6
9:30pm – 1:00am	**Dance to the Sounds of the Manila Diamonds.** Meet the Ambassador Hosts and enjoy an evening of dancing in our Crystal Ballroom!	Club 2100	6
9:45pm – 10:30pm	**Tom Daniels** entertains at the piano during after-dinner cocktails.	Crystal Cove	5
10:00pm – Late	**Disco Dancing.** D. J. Dante spins the sounds of today and yesterday.	Stars Lounge	6

One Show Only This Evening at 10:15pm

WELCOME ABOARD PRESENTATION

Presenting "PIRATES TO PINAFORE"

performed by the Crystal Ensemble of Singers and Dancers:

Featuring Lead Vocalists **ROBERT YACKO**

AND **MELINA KALOMAS**

Valeri Ovtcharov • Brian Webster • Vincent Cuny

Alexander Forster • Nicola Goncalves

Emma Wilkinson • Catherine Hoskins • Lisa Blunt

Followed by Cruise Director Paul McFarland,
who will introduce some of his key personnel with a special dance
presentation by dance champions Audrey and Jim Applegate.

accompanied by **The Galaxy Orchestra** directed by Vincent Laurentis

GALAXY LOUNGE

Due to International copyright law, videotaping of production shows is forbidden.

Paul's Late Night Smile – Dear Lord, please make me the person my dog thinks I am.

Crystal Harmony • Monday, August 13, 2001

Example - Daily Program Back

Each evening during dinner, the cabin steward/ess will leave the Daily Program for the next day. As your night ends, take time to read it carefully to determine if and when there is a dance class tomorrow, pre-dinner or pre-show dancing and what the hours are for the regular evening dancing. You'll then be able to plan each of your days to get the most from the activities being offered.

Learn who the cruise director, maitre d'hôtel, hotel manager are and say hello when you see them. The maitre d'hôtel is responsible for the entire dining room. You'll meet him there when you first arrive to be seated for dinner, and that will usually be the extent of your contact with him. The other officers are introduced at the Captain's reception, which is normally the second night of the cruise. Know who these folks are and realize that they are continually busy. They'll make the overture to talk to you when they have an interest or need. Otherwise, be friendly, but don't take their time. Be available to them if and when they need your help.

Chapter 25 - DINING

For the evening meal, you'll be assigned to a specific dinner table by the maitre d'hôtel. This man is a professional and frequently adjusts table setups to help the guests enjoy their dining experience. Determine from the other hosts whether dinner tables are assigned the first or second night of the cruise. When there are introductions the first night of the cruise, the welcome aboard show schedule may not allow time for a normal dinner. In this case, all of the hosts may eat together at the early dinner seating. Specific table assignments will be made the following night. On some ships the hosts sit together throughout each cruise.

Typically, as the maitre d'hôtel puts his dining room together, there evolve a few tables of six or eight with several single women. These are where hosts are normally assigned on the elite ships. When this is the system, each host needs to check with the maitre d' the second evening to get a permanent table assignment if that wasn't done the first night. Hosts normally join the same table for dinner each evening of the cruise.

In some cases, hosts may be rotated between seatings and perhaps among tables. In that case, periodically, each host will greet and get acquainted with another group of guests. Should the cruise be one where hosts are rotated, follow the directions of the person coordinating the host activities. The maitre d'hôtel will make the initial table assignment, but will not have the time to help you beyond that. Be sure you understand the process of where to be and when from the other hosts or dance instructors.

It's permissible to occasionally accept invitations to join other guests at alternative dining rooms. Acceptance or declination should be gracious. Acceptance should be made sufficiently in advance so you can tell the normal table waiter and table-mates when you'll be absent. Once you're assigned to a table, be there on time. When I first join a table, I explain that my duties will sometimes require me to finish my meal rapidly so I can be available for a scheduled function. For example, perhaps everyone at my table is not seated until 6:45 pm, but I have to be at pre-show dancing by 8 pm. Hence, my time for dinner is compressed by 45 minutes. Normally, everyone is very understanding. They appreciate knowing early on that I'll occasionally have to eat and run.

As you develop camaraderie at your table, you'll find it to be an excellent public relations arena. This is one of the best places you'll have to be sure that everyone has the opportunity to talk about him/her-self, their interests, and past as well as future trips. It's a good idea to buy a bottle of wine for the table on the third and the next to the last nights of the cruise, assuming you have a liquor allowance. More about that allowance later.

There will be occasions when seating in the dining room will be open, such as some breakfasts and lunches. Open seating typically allows everyone to be seated wherever and with whomever the waiter doing the seating indicates. These are great opportunities to invite a group of ladies to dine with you.

Chapter 26 - PUNCTUALITY

When there is a dance class, scheduled dancing, or special activity with dancing, be in the designated room ready to work ahead of time. The rule is to be where you're expected at least five minutes ahead of the activity's published time! That way, you're still on time when "they" move the function to another location and fail to tell you. There may be some new or different plans that everyone needs to know before the activity gets going. Shipboard activities begin and end on time, and dancing is one of the most visible.

Chapter 27 - FEATURE APPEARANCES

The Uniform Events. For introduction events, the hosts will dress in the assignments' uniform (usually a navy blazer, white pants, socks and white dress shoes). Be sure to wear your name tag.

The formal introduction. Either on the first or third night, sometimes both, the cruise director will introduce the hosts to all the guests during the evening show after dinner. One of the experienced hosts or the cruise director should let you know when and where to sit and then stand for introduction to the audience. The cruise director may simply have the hosts stand to be recognized, or he may invite them on stage and even ask them to introduce themselves. If asked to say hello, make yours short no matter what the others do. Give them your name, where your home is, and a sound byte that will help them to remember you. Keep the entire introduction to less than 12 seconds. Always have a couple of planned introductions and practiced sound bytes ready for delivery. They'll serve you well when people say, "Hi, who are you?"

The singles cocktail party. On some ships the cruise director may make or repeat the introduction of the hosts at the Singles Cocktail Party. It is usually held during the third day of the cruise. This party is announced in the daily program. It may be a casual afternoon event warranting only dress slacks and a solid colored shirt. A pre-dinner dance affair with various staff members attending would require the uniform for hosts. Either way, this is the function for the single guests to get acquainted. By now you may have already gotten to know a number of these ladies. Use the opportunity to see whom you've missed and get acquainted with them, too. Make the most of it and have fun! Notice if there are any single men present, and if so whether they dance. The single men who dance should always be given the opportunity to ask a lady to dance before the hosts extend an invitation.

The Formal Events. Typically on a seven-day cruise there are two formal affairs given for all the guests—one at the beginning of the cruise and one at the end. Hosts wear a complete black tuxedo to both of these functions. Since these are receptions for all the guests, there is one party for the early seating and another for those on the main dinner seating. When there is dancing provided, all the hosts are expected to attend both events and to dance with the guests. The receptions normally begin 45 minutes before each dinner seating and will end at the time the guests would normally go to the dining room to begin their evening of dining**Error! Bookmark not defined.** and entertainment. Since the early seating hosts (the first team) have to be at the second party when it begins, they'll have little time for dinner. When that's your situation, tell the waiter and the guests at your table that this is one of those rushed evenings. The waiter can get you served quickly and out on time. The second team will have their normal meal after the party for the main seating guests.

The first of these formal affairs is the Captain's welcome aboard party, held the second day of the cruise. This is traditionally the dressier of the formal nights. The Captain personally welcomes the guests into the party, will have champagne served, and on the elite ships, he'll make dancing

Formal - Black Tux

available. He'll briefly introduce some of the key officers responsible for the ship. During the Captain's portion of the reception, move to the back of the room out of the way of the guests.

The second reception for all the guests will be the Captain's farewell party, typically on the next to last evening of the cruise. The Captain will again welcome the guests to enjoy champagne, dancing and formally wish everyone a safe journey home. Either he or the cruise director may take just a minute to acknowledge the hosts. The cruise director will let you know where to be if such an acknowledgment is going to take place. That location should be somewhere close to the dance floor within eyesight of the cruise director. Otherwise, move to the back of the room so you don't block the view of the guests.

There may be one other formal affair. That's when the cruise line sponsors a reception for those guests who have previously traveled with the Company. Since it's intended only for repeaters, it's an invitation-only party, and there is usually only one activity scheduled. Otherwise, it's very much the same type of an affair as the two Captain's parties. It may be staffed by the cruise director and the social host(ess), who represent the cruise line rather than the just the ship. This may or may not be a formal affair. It may or may not be an evening affair. It will normally not be announced in the daily program. Since it's an invitation-only affair, the hosts should receive a written invitation. Check the time carefully, since it may conflict with part of your scheduled dinner time—another one of those abbreviated meals. If the **Repeater's Party** is a form-al affair, hosts wear a white jacket with their tuxedo in place of the black jacket.

Other Than Captain's Receptions

Chapter 28 - SHIPBOARD ACTIVITIES

Every cruise is different and full of programs available for everyone's entertainment. Hosts should attend as many of the daytime functions as they like. These are both informative and good opportunities for socializing with guests who might otherwise be missed. For example:

Games: Bridge players abound. If you like to play, just show up at the announced times and you're in. If you don't play the game or are a beginner or novice, feel free to attend the lessons. After awhile, you may be able to get a group together to play. You and many of the guests may prefer to play rummy or hearts, etc.

A lot of folks enjoy playing board games like backgammon or scrabble. These could provide a good opportunity to have a guest teach you. Table tennis is always fun and, for the energetic, there is often an equipped paddle tennis court.

Bingo: This and related games for prizes are generally off limits. The Rule: Hosts may never compete with passengers for winnings, position, etc. Keep this in mind when deciding whether or not to participant with guests in some of the games mentioned above.

Casino: Naturally, a host may gamble in the casino since it's against a common house. *Be aware,* however, that your active participation will be noticed. Believe it or not, even this can create unsuspected problems. Greed can do amazing things. Just clean out a slot machine that one of the guests has pumped a couple of hundred dollars into and imagine what their feelings about you might be. There are several similar reasons which lead me to forego these activities.

Dance:
Lessons
Hosts' attendance is mandatory. When dance instructors are aboard the ship, they'll teach a complimentary dance lesson when the ship is at sea. Attend every session, enthusiastically, and do what the instructors teach, even if you know it differently or won't ever use it. That's part of being a supportive team member. Invite all the ladies to come and join the group. You might even have the opportunity to improve your own material. Recall the discussion in chapter 6 about dancing?

Chapter 29 - BAR CREDIT

As a host, it's appropriate to buy drinks for friends and for the entertainment of the unaccompanied guests. When a bar credit is provided to hosts, it's *for such social use*, not personal consumption. The credit has a daily limit and is intended for the host to at least buy an occasional bottle of wine for his dinner table. One host whom I admire greatly offers wine for his table with "compliments from the ship," since he doesn't drink alcohol.

Any amount charged above the credit limit will be billed to the host. The efficient ships will send each host a letter specifying the amount of the credit. The concierge or dance instructors can help you get the details if need be. Find out *before* you start picking up tabs.

Warning! It's usual for a lot of alcohol to be consumed on a ship. Regardless of the circumstances, a host must know and stay within his limit as drinking can clearly affect his performance as a host and dancer. That's why most dancers drink water. When improper or excessive consumption of alcohol is noticeable, it is grounds for discharge from the ship.

Chapter 30 - PORTS

A significant part of the cruise experience is enjoying the exotic ports of call the cruise lines visit in their worldwide itineraries. A host can always go ashore on his own and explore as a tourist. Often the shore excursion staff can help point him toward interesting places.

As discussed in chapter 14—Personal Expenses—the further away from North America you go, the less often you'll find merchants, taxis, cyber cafes and pay telephones that accept American money. This is frustrating when all you want to buy is a few postcards or a cup of coffee, but that's the way it is. Recently, I was with a group touring a beautiful temple filled with Chinese New Year activities in Taipei, Taiwan. We'd left the ship immediately upon arrival for a full day of exploring the treasures of the area, so the only money I had was American and Japanese. Sadly, the little shop in the temple wouldn't accept either of my currencies or credit cards. Hence, no transaction could be made. I found throughout that part of the world that credit cards were accepted only in the large hotels and those stores that cater to international visitors. Those were often not where I found the truly interesting souvenirs.

Changing money in port may be a problem. In many cases, there will be neither the availability nor the time to find money-changing facilities. If you didn't buy the various currencies, as suggested in chapter 14, you can check with the ship's concierge about any arrangements they may have for the guests to purchase local currencies en route. Don't be disappointed if they're not able to help.

Warning: When you exchange money along the way, always get a printed receipt for the transaction. Get it or cancel the transaction immediately. Take the time, then and there, to verify that you were given all the money the receipt indicated you should have received. Sometimes the exchanger will fail to give you all the coins that should have been part of the transaction. Commissions and fees are noted on the receipt. They are deducted from the amount before the total you should receive is printed.

Make a mental note that none of the currency exchanges worldwide will accept and convert coins of any currency. If you've exchanged US$50 into a foreign currency and then want to convert it back to American money, only the bills from the foreign currency will be accepted and exchanged. An alternative to converting money back is to find someone who will be returning to that country—guests, crew, etc.—and sell it to them. Everyone wins since no one pays another commission.

Chapter 31 - SHORE EXCURSIONS

The ships with the best host programs offer the gentlemen opportunities to join or to escort some of the shore excursions. Find out what the policy is from the other hosts if you weren't told by your booking agent. When escorting is part of the activities, tactfully contact the shore excursion staff early in the cruise if they don't contact you first. Inquire about the procedure for volunteering to escort tours. Make this contact when there are no guests around, and be courteous. Don't ever put the excursion staff in an uncomfortable place since they already have a tough enough job.

When escorting is available, it's an opportunity extended to the hosts in addition to many of the crew and staff. Hence, you'll compete with a number of other people for any assignment. Seniority of the applicants is often the assignment criterion since those folks have been bypassed or have helped the staff solve tough situations most often over time. When assigned as an escort, you're expected to assist with any problems that arise and report your impressions after the tour.

If there is an excursion that you really want to take, don't gamble on escorting it. Purchase a ticket and enjoy it along with the guests. Given the limited number of assignments, there will be many times when there is not one for you. Don't be offended or feel that you have been deliberately overlooked. Your reaction may be no different from the feelings a lady experiences when she feels you haven't given her a fair share of the dances. Use the space as your time aboard the ship or possibly to do some creative touristering on your own.

If you've developed a good friendship with the excursion staff, when there are no guests around, ask them about on shore activities. Some of these may not be available to the guests. If you do hit a winner in one of these unscheduled adventures, don't arouse the resentment of the guests by impressing them with it. Be careful not to commit to any assignments or other activities that are energy drains. They could make an evening of mandatory dancing tough to do.

TIPS WHEN ASSISTING ONSHORE EXCURSIONS:

1. Be at the assigned bus or boat at the time specified. That will be before the guests begin disembarking the ship. Learn your tour guide's name. Verify that the tour will cover all, and be limited to, the program published by the ship.

2. Have the guests give their tickets to the guide as they board.

3. Once everyone is aboard and the guide is ready to go, ask to use the microphone to:
   a) introduce yourself as the escort from the ship,
   b) make sure the microphone is working and that you can be understood,
   c) help the guests recognize that you're there to help them enjoy the excursion,
   d) tell them to notify you and the guide if they decide to leave the tour, and finally,
   e) introduce the tour guide by name.

4. Take a head count as you walk to your seat at the back of the bus. Write the number down. Confirm it at each stop on the tour before the bus proceeds. The tour guide will look to you before traveling on. Your count is critical. I was escorting a bus visiting two different art museums in Cannes, France. Preparing to leaving the Chagall site, I was one person short. The man had left his purchases on his seat and told the driver that he was walking to the other museum which was not more than a mile up the road. We went on with the tour on schedule. The man never reappeared, which made keeping this activity wrinkle-free for the rest of the guests a bit tricky. When we returned to the ship, I took his things to the excursion desk and found out that he'd decided not to finish the tour and had taken a cab back to the ship an hour-and-a-half earlier.

5. Leave the seats at the front of the bus for the guests. Escorts sit in the back. Here is the feat of the day. Just prior to the bus stopping for a walking tour or a photo stop, the escort must walk to the

steps at the back door. If there isn't one, beat it to the front door. Either way, he/she will be the first person off to lend a helping hand to the guests. You are off-the-hook when there is no back door, and the driver chooses to help the folks. Be sure to hold on to the overhead aisles railings to steady and brace yourself as you walk to the door since the bus will still be moving. It's a good idea to work this out with the tour guide before starting the tour. You'll need to be the last person back aboard so you can complete the headcount and verify that everyone has returned before letting the bus move.

6. The tour manager likes to see the escorts keeping the group together as much as possible while on foot. By staying a bit ahead of the slow walkers, you can encourage them to keep the pace. Know which way and where the guide has gone so you can point stragglers in the correct direction. Don't get lost yourself.

7. It's essential that you know what not to do should a guest in your group get sick or injured. Do nothing which would appear that you could or would take on the responsibility of treating or caring for them. Do offer customary assistance and support for the person. It's the tour company's responsibility to have them handled and taken care of. Neither stay behind nor leave with the person. As an escort, you are there to assist with the group. They remain your charge until a responsible ship official instructs you otherwise. Do get the person's cabin number and make a note of what happened, when, and what treatment was offered. After the tour, confirm the person's name and cabin number with the people at the reception desk. Leave a record of what happened for the ship's excursions office.

8. At the end of the tour, you'll need to be the last person off the bus. That way *you* will be able to make a final search of the seats and racks making sure that no one left anything. If someone did leave something, take it with you, tell the guide you have it and turn it in at the reception desk. Report any problems to the excursion office.

Chapter 32 - YOUR FRIENDS

From the minute you arrive at a resort or on a ship, you're surrounded by people wanting to be your friends. In many cases, they'll even be interested in actually getting to know you. They begin with the first person you meet upon arrival and will pop up everywhere else. Many of them are employees; since hosts are not really guests, they can experience you as one of them. After awhile, the importance of those friendships will become clearer. First, these men and women will actually help take care of you. Second, they're the only ones who'll continue to be there week after week as the guests come and go. They'll value your friendship because you're not part of the staffing circle, and yet you don't disappear like everyone else. These people begin at the front door.

The Bellman

When I was dancing at a Ritz Hotel regularly, Byron opened the car door and parked my car for me. We soon started chatting while the car was being brought around. That broke the ice for later conversations when he was abandoning bachelorhood, had photos of one and then two children and then decided to change careers. All of this made my arrivals and departures feel more than first class. On a ship, this person is one of the staff who oversees the use of the gangways.

Concierge and Reception

These are great people. Their role is indispensable for a smooth vacation since they're on the front lines dealing with everyone who has problems. When they're able to connect with another human being with a positive outlook, it helps make their world a bit easier to live in. One of those days way down the line when you're feeling under par, having one or two of these friends to talk with will make more sense. When they like and respect you, they're in the place to help with that occasional special request. After I'd worked this one resort for a couple of years and had produced good feedback from many of the guests, I was flattered by the extra consideration my requests received. The same has been equally true on the ships.

109

Shore Excursion

We've already discussed the importance of being well liked and known by the shore excursion people. Since they're acutely aware of the power position they're in, they're wary of any host who is overly friendly. It's rare for anyone to whom they can offer an assignment to develop the type of friendship that I've mentioned above. Know who each of them is and be genuinely friendly when you see them. Be helpful when given the opportunity, but otherwise treat them as you do the other executive staff. Let them call you when they need to.

Bar Staff

The bar staff should always be among your best friends. These people, like a host, have to always be "on," so they sympathize with you. They're also wonderfully helpful when they accept you as one of them. I do several things in the nightclub to make it easy for them to work with me. First, I sit in the same place all the time. Second, I order the same thing from them all the time. Since they quickly learn my schedule, when I walk in to begin dancing, my order is at my seat waiting for me. Even new servers have the process down pat in a night or two, and they never let me run out. These folks work hard and truly go that extra mile which we're all striving to do for those around us. I periodically leave a small cash tip in appreciation for their effectiveness. Consistency is the key to achieving this rapport, and you control that.

The same holds true in other facilities like the coffee shop. Many of the folks working there are just as genuine as the reception staff, and equally sensitive to the slick operator. When you develop the human attitude discussed in chapter 7, you'll have the ability to truly meet these people, too. Even though your request is always taken care of after those from the guests, which is the way it is, the feeling of visiting friends makes the time special. All of these people are among the sharpest in the world at spotting lushes and slick operators, and they handle them with the grace of a diplomat. When they find the real thing returning to visit them, they're willing to share a whole different world with that person. Consistency, again, helps them effectively respond to you.

Musicians

Although there are many other people on the ship interested in your friendship, another group that needs special attention is the band that you dance to every night. Most of them will never make an effort to get acquainted with you, let alone say hello. They'll almost universally function as their own little clique. They figure that they're just the band whom everyone sees as an animated jukebox. Whoever goes over and talks to the jukebox when it's been turned off? I try to get to know these human beings too, since they make the world I live in every night. If the sambas and cha-chas are too fast, if the waltzes and tangos are too slow, or if the night is full of viennese waltzes, we still have to dance to every one of them. Can you imagine their reaction to the "experts" who are all to happy to go out of their way to tell the "jukebox" how the stuff should be played?

On the other hand, when these folks truly like you, they'll be understanding of your few requests. Then, spending an evening with them is like spending a marvelous evening dancing to your favorite music being played for you by friends. That changes the entire atmosphere of the ballroom and the dances you share.

SUMMARY

When the significant aspects of chapter 7 produce the attitude of a genuine human being in a host, then all the payoffs described in this chapter will happen automatically. These hosts are the best of the best. They enjoy what they're doing. They're naturally sensitive to those around them and set themselves aside to help others be significant. These are the men who get the greatest fulfillment from every assignment. Hopefully, this **map** will help you discover those treasures each day.

Chapter 33 - SOCIAL SKILL IN ACTION

What happened? How did we end up back at this topic while learning about life at sea? It's not unusual, when at a resort or on a ship, for hosts to lose track of the basics of their role. They forget that they have a multi-faceted job to do; that they're not "guests." Though dancing remains a rather obvious expectation, the clarity of the social responsibility diminishes to a point of nonexistence—except in the best.

I had taken the shuttle being used to move guests and crew from the ship to a resort town, Vine del Mare, in Chile this hot, humid summer day. I was on my own time along with everyone else and was tired, having completed my shopping. Being mid-afternoon, many of the crew who had been enjoying some time off needed to get back to the ship. A lot of guests were also waiting for the bus. When those on the arriving coach were offloaded, the crew waited until the guests were aboard, and then they took whatever seats were available. Before we could leave, more guests boarded the bus. Crew members and musicians immediately got out of the seats they had found and moved to the back of the bus so smoothly that everyone felt comfortable and honored. It's not often that a large number of employees demonstrate the natural traits that we hosts frequently seem to forget. Hosts and staff are there to be sure the guests feel special.

Social Graces

A few other obvious and noticed practices of the gracious gentleman include the following. These and many other natural courtesies are part of what creates a host's image.

- When you're out in the public areas, notice who's there. Ask to sit with some of the unaccompanied guests or others whom you haven't yet befriended.
- Open or hold doors for guests, allowing them to go first.
- Stand and handle a lady's chair to seat her when the opportunity presents itself.

- ✦ Stand up whenever a guest joins you or a group of people that you're sitting with. Do the same when they leave you.
- ✦ Get the server's or shop clerk's attention for the ladies when the need arises.
- ✦ Allow the ladies at the table to start the eating process.
- ✦ After a dance, escort the lady back to her seat, group or friend with your arm or holding hers, and thank her for the dance. Do not leave her standing at the edge of the dance floor or halfway down the aisle to reach for another lady. See the next chapter on dance protocol.

Guests have an unprecedented penchant, as onlookers, to continually notice what hosts are doing. They recognized the crew's behavior in the above bus episode. On the negative side, they'll notice the host who 1) doesn't do his share of dancing with all the ladies, 2) doesn't extend the above common courtesies, 3) spends too much time talking with other hosts, and 4) acts indifferently toward the guests or staff. Many will conclude that the guy shouldn't be a host since he appears to be either unqualified for the role or a freeloader on a free cruise. They'll comment to others during the cruise and their evaluations will reflect those observations.

Handling Problems or Complaints

Hosts are not staff. Hence, they can't do much when graced by the complaints or problems of either the ladies or guests. Here's the predicament. Once a host has listened earnestly to their problem, he's taken on the responsibility to personally help them resolve it. That's fine when fixing it is easy to do. For example, those times when the host can alter his immediate activity to escort the guest(s) to the venue they can't find, like the movie theater or the card room. It's a different story when they're complaining about everything else, including the host. In those cases, don't take the comments personally. Do direct the individual to someone who can help. Escort them or pleasantly direct them to the proper staff such as those at the reception desk or the head waiter. A truly professional touch is to follow-up on the issue the next time they're around to be sure they felt taken care of satisfactorily.

Avoid the company of those who are complainers. If caught and unable to excuse yourself, then listen sympathetically. Hopefully, something in the conversation will provide a bridge to a pleasant or neutral subject. Remember, you're not staff so it's best to plead ignorance about the company, even if you have personal knowledge or feelings one way or the other. At the same time, do nothing which would be disloyal to the agent you may be representing, the cruise director, other entertainers or the company. Don't become defensive!

If the conversation is dealing with real issues related to the cruise, simply direct the guest(s) to the proper staff where their complaining may do some good. These folks are known for doing a good job dealing with real issues and the people presenting them, even if they're people who just can't be satisfied. Stay out of harm's way, and simply listen.

When it comes to the food, entertainment, music, dancing and all of the other components of the environment, quality is an individually biased matter. You, I, and they have had far different experiences with all these things as well as the events surrounding the moment. Perception and personal taste come from a lifetime of unique experiences which produce each person's opinion. You may find that the food or entertainment, or what have you, is not to your liking. Understand that these things may vary with the caliber of the resort or ship. On the elite ships, the guests' amenities are above average and are well received by the majority of travelers. Clearly correctable problems should be made known to the proper staff members so they can do their jobs.

Any negative opinions you have about the food, the entertainment, or the service must be kept to yourself. These things are not to be discussed in any way outside your cabin. If discussed at all, they can't get back to guests or staff. When you return home, send a letter with your opinions to the resort, the cruise line or the agent who was responsible for your assignment if you wish.

The Surprise
This applies to people on cruises longer than seven days. The phenomenon doesn't seem to occur at resorts since so few people are there for an extended period of time.

You'll find that everyone has adjusted easily to the food, the entertainment, and the dancing. Everything is going as smoothly as possible. The ladies are responding well to you and everyone's dancing has smoothed out. The routine is becoming second nature and relaxed. Then, all of a sudden there are bickering, complaining, and frustrating events that erupt from nowhere. What happened? You entered the 10th or 11th day of the trip. This is a break point in 14-day and longer cruises. It's the rare cruise when the majority of ladies on trips of these lengths remain content and happy. Boredom, competition, disappointment and the routine produce their subterranean discord, which will manifest as dissatisfaction with the utopian world you're in.

Beware of the envious, controlling, empire-building hosts who contribute to this discord. Their ego needs get them embroiled in the camps that may evolve. Stay above these troubled waters, and don't get involved in back-stabbing or gossiping with anyone. Your comments will get back to the wrong people with your name attached.

As a diplomat, these are the most important times to review and reset your attitude. That way you'll be able to listen to and pleasantly accept those having a tough time. Often, all they need is some compassionate support. When you do those things, you'll be amazed how everyone snaps back to their cheerful nature without turning against you as the cruise comes to an end.

Chapter 34 - DANCING PROTOCOL

On the job, the first concern a host has every day is to determine when and where the dance activities will take place. Everyone receives a schedule of daily events that includes these activities. Resorts often publish this as a weekly schedule of events. Cruise ships distribute a detailed schedule in the evening for the following day - see chapter 24. Hosts carefully read the program each evening to determine when and where they are expected to dance throughout the following day. They look to see if someone slipped dancing into the afternoon tea time or on the main stage preceding the evening show. Is there a dance class or, surprise, two during the day? It's a given that when there are dance classes scheduled, a host's attendance is **mandatory**. Once you're out there dancing the ladies for real, the following points will be important.

- **Being On Time**

Each host is responsible for finding the dance activities in the schedule for each day. He's expected to be in the right place properly dressed and on time. On time means: **being where he's expected to be at least five minutes ahead of time!** Hosts must get there earlier so they are still on time when the function is moved to another location and nobody tells them. I've worked with several resident instructors who expected the hosts to be present and ready to dance ten minutes before class was scheduled to begin. Why? These instructors played music before class so everyone could review the material they learned in the previous class. Suddenly, there's reason for each host to have learned and remembered that material since they are now responsible for leading the ladies through it.

- **You're On Duty**

Often the evening dancing will go on until 1 a.m., which will signal the end of a host's day. What a host does after that is his choice. However, if he goes to the disco, or anywhere else, he's still a host and all of the rules still apply. He's not off duty. Again, beware of the onlookers among the staff as well as the guests.

Always talk with the other hosts or the resident instructors about dancing after hours. On more than one occasion the cruise director has responded by extending the end of the evening's dancing. His logic was A...since the hosts appeared to want and were willing to do more, then formalize it...A

● **Getting Off the Dance Floor**

Equally important is the ground rule that hosts don't dance with anyone for any reason during the band's break time. There is often recorded dance music playing during these breaks, and some ladies will want to dance to it. They fail to recognize that these are the host's recuperation breaks. Wise uses of these times include visiting the men's room, relaxing away from the dancing venue, sitting down with one person or group that they haven't already spent some social time with, etc.

● **Instructing**

Another well-established rule that was touched on before is that the hosts don't teach dance lessons. You'll say, "Right, makes sense to me." Then when the music has stopped playing, or heaven forbid, when the band has left the stage on a break, you find yourself standing there on the dance floor with some drop-dead gorgeous young lady. You've finally gotten to dance with her and feel that you must show her how to do a step or answer her question about one. Guess what the dance instructors, ladies, and onlookers are going to think if you don't disappear immediately! A word to the wise: get off the dance floor when the music has stopped playing and deal with her elsewhere.

● **"Fixing" a Lady's Dancing**

Related to this instructing rule is a more rude behavior and a proven host-killer. That is fixing the lady or her dancing while sharing a piece of music during one of the scheduled activities. Keep in mind that the dance music is provided for everyone to enjoy dancing socially to the best of their ability. My mother traveled with a private agent who booked hosted dance cruises after I started dancing with them and was a stern teacher for me. When she and I would dance she never hesitated to say, "Cut out that fancy stuff, sonny, when you

117

dance with your mother." Her point and the invaluable lesson? Each of the ladies is there to have a good time doing what they can do. The best hosts figure out what the lady can enjoy doing and make that meaningful. It's just that simple.

I recently danced a moderately fast hustle with a lovely elderly lady. This sweetheart was losing her eyesight, and had trouble walking even when the ship was docked. Still, when asked, she said, "Sure, let's do it." She couldn't move fast enough to do hustle steps even if she knew the footwork, which she didn't. If she turned at all, it was with too many steps and me praying she wouldn't lose her balance. Yet, she walked proudly off the floor after dancing the entire thing saying she loved it, and she probably enjoyed doing it more than I did. Did we talk about what she should do? No. Did I push her into a hustle? No. We did little more than a single step swing basic and a couple of cuddles. She could do all of that to the rhythm being played and knew that she'd been dancing.

- ● **Who Dances**
  Again, hosts are present to dance with the unaccompanied ladies. When a lady is present with an escort, she's obviously not unaccompanied. Hence, she's not among the group of guests to be approached or invited to dance. The only time a host would approach an accompanied lady is when her escort has invited him to dance with her. He should let the other hosts know that her escort has asked that she be danced with. Even then, use discretion and don't overly monopolize her time since she's there to share the experience with her escort. I watch hosts deliberately ask attractive, escorted ladies to dance while leaving unaccompanied ladies from the focus group sitting. Then I listen to those same guys complain about getting poor evaluations. Are you surprised? Keep in mind that: 1) you don't want her companion to become envious or jealous, and 2) you don't want the ever-present onlookers to watch you slighting the unaccompanied ladies.

One other group of guests to keep in mind is the unattached gentlemen. There won't be more than three of them on the ship who show up to dance. However, when there are unattached gentlemen guests or staff wanting to dance, the hosts "stand down." It may be necessary for the hosts to wait a short time after the band has started playing a piece to allow these men to get there first. The rule: the guests come and go first.

The focus remains on ladies older than 55 who are traveling alone, but not to the exclusion of the 7-year-olds and all of those in between. Hosts must be consciously impartial, socially as well as on the dance floor, spreading their time and attention equitably among all the unaccompanied ladies.

Many of the women in the focus group will be widowed or divorced, some recently. Hence, their self-esteem may not be particularly good. Many of this group were raised not to be socially assertive. Regardless, the host initiates contact and invites the lady to dance. If as a host you don't, you'll find many of these folks becoming self conscious wondering why you asked the other women, but not them. At a minimum, they'll feel slighted. Don't let that happen.

The objective for each man is to maintain the image of equality without partiality in the eyes of everyone. Otherwise, even the other hosts will become opinionated onlookers. The role of host includes the social privilege of an ambassador. Meaning: be friendly, but keep moving along to dance with or speak to the next lady or group of ladies during the evenings. Done consistently, with style and grace, this will keep the host free from entrapment and the appearance of partiality. Even if a host doesn't flirt with the troubles discussed back in the chapter on romance, he can create the illusion of it. To stay out of troubled waters, hosts monitor their feelings and behavior. They don't let feelings bond them with those ladies they're attracted to. They are especially careful with the ladies who are obviously more attractive, better dancers, and more interesting to be around.

● **Being a Dancer**

Hosts are not there to show themselves off. Mom would say, "Cut it out, sonny." Hosts are there to help each of the ladies they dance with have a good time doing what they can do, showing them off to the extent possible. Part of the magic each host should be able to perform is knowing how to use the spectrum of ballroom dance materials well enough to make each lady feel comfortable, as if she were a graceful Ginger Rogers, each time she leaves the dance floor with him. Like many of the other hosts, had I picked out a woman

119

who could keep up with my hustle, the lady a couple of paragraphs ago would probably not have danced. She deserved equal attention.

Regardless of their danceability, the ladies aren't attending any dance activity to be criticized or corrected. They're there to have fun and to leave the dance floor feeling successful and happy—even if they can't dance by some people's standards. The ship doesn't provide the bands, dance floors, and hosts simply for trained or good dancers. They're provided for guests of all ages and capabilities to have fun dancing as part of their vacation. Hosts are provided to make that happen particularly for the focus group. It's incumbent on each host to have sufficient knowledge and skill to dance down or up or differently to each lady's level of ability. The men are not there to draw attention to her frame, dance position, or form of movement.

Out of any group of ladies that converge to dance, there will be those who move better than others and are more stimulating to be with. Watch out! This signals one of those booby traps. Hosts must be careful not to let these ladies dominate their attention, on or off the dance floor. By paying attention to their feelings, a man will detect the signal indicating it's time to go look for the shyer and less capable ladies. Be sure these women are getting their fair share, and get back to them a bit more often. Just as in his own home, a host must be on the lookout for those needing extra attention or encouragement to join in. Interact with them in a fashion that makes getting involved comfortable for them.

As dancing to the same music for weeks at a time becomes routine, it's normal for one to feel they've earned the right to sit out a dance, or to just simply run and hide, occasionally. The latter is one way to spend 15 minutes out of each hour, when the band takes a break. Otherwise, the guests expect the hosts to be there to dance, not sit around and chat. In fact, the people who commiserate with a gentleman about his situation in the coffee shop will be the same ones who will expect to see him dancing whenever the band is playing. What do you think they and other people say when they see a host sit and talk with a lady through the entire break, and then head for the door as the band starts playing again? Walk out the door to go to the restroom or to do anything else during a set and these folks will 1) notice that a host skipped out during dance time, and 2) see him as avoiding dancing. It's not unusual to spot the same guy(s) doing this frequently during a cruise.

Leaving the room is not the way for a host to catch his breath. A better method is to occasionally take time to walk to the back of and around the room. It's not unusual to find that a shier lady has slipped in unnoticed yet hoping that some how someone will find her. Learning to pace himself on the dance floor is important.

The best hosts help create a gracious environment by moving off the floor and consciously deciding whose turn it is for the next piece that's just starting. They *don't* stand or hover around the ladies like vultures once they've escorted a lady to her seat after a dance. Use this time to get out of the way and take a sip of water or whatever. It's ok to hear what the band is going to play before deciding whether to stay in strict rotation or to mix dances around a little. Very near the beginning of the piece, approach and ask the lady to dance. On a recent cruise, a lovely lady who was a good dancer commented, "That waltz we were doing was really too slow." The next time it was my turn to dance with her, another slow waltz was played, so I skipped her for that dance. I returned to her for the next dance, which was a cha-cha, and everyone was happy. Just be sure that all the ladies get equal attention and consideration. When the hosts don't work the rooms that way, watch what happens. When a lady feels left out or ignored, she'll start writing down who dances how many times with whom, and report the results to the cruise director when they don't balance. Don't let your name get on one of those lists.

- **Hygiene**

It's surprising that there are people who aren't aware of the odors that their body gives off, especially in this close contact sport. Dancing is a physical activity and it may well make a person perspire. Since dancing is such an intimate activity, it's good manners to bathe and to apply deodorant to various bodily parts before heading to the dance floor. This is true whether going to a lesson or an evening of dancing. Please, don't inflict your personal aromas, including strong perfumes, tainted breath or sunbathed body on others!

Many of the lady dancers use some kind of hand lotion. Avoid these lotions for yourself as they make it difficult to hold on to your partner and will also stain, and possibly ruin, your partner's clothing.

vanLee Hughey

You'll discover that it isn't a pleasant feeling to have your partner's hands "slip sliding away" just about the time you need the contact.

Chapter 35 - APPLAUSE OR CRUCIFIXION

As each cruise comes to an end, a quality rating form is left in each of the guest cabins. This is the guest's assessment and feedback device used by the cruise line to evaluate how its people and programs are being received. There are sections for rating each of the guests' facilities as well as the entertainment. Each of the hosts is identified for rating by all the guests, not just the ladies with whom they had the opportunity to dance. The vast majority of those on the cruise will choose the Not Applicable or Not Used category. However, each host can rest assured that those guests on whom they made an impression, positive or negative, will complete this section of the form. Many of these guests will have been the onlookers mentioned throughout the book. That's exactly how it should be. You'll remember from chapter 1 that the host's role encompasses all the guests.

Reflect for a minute about how you've completed similar rating forms. How did you form your opinion of those you were writing up? Would you expect people to primarily identify those things done well or to identify those things they felt were inappropriate, offensive, or should be done better? The key word is "felt." Fortunately, a lot of people who go luxury cruising watch for, recognize, and are anxious to rate and praise good performance. Since hosts are highly visible to all the guests both on the ship and off, they can count on being rated by as many onlookers as unaccompanied ladies with whom they've danced. However, even those ladies will have been onlookers a good deal of the time. They, too, will report how they felt about what they saw.

When an onlooker forms a quick, unfavorable impression of a host, it will normally be at one of the special scheduled functions. It will be difficult for that host to redeem himself because the onlooker probably won't be present at other dance functions. When they do return to dance or to listen to the music, they may be swayed back to at least a neutral position if they like what they see and hear. Then again, should they believe you're slighting a lady, playing favorites, or behaving improperly, they'll go so far as to write down their impressions. To recap, some of those notable impression include being late for a dance, dancing with accompanied ladies while others sit, showing disproportionate attention to some lady(s), and sitting around talking rather than dancing when music is playing. Dance cheek-to-cheek with the same young, attractive lady more than once during a cruise, and watch what happens!

There are several things which can be inferred from the rest of this book that you can do throughout an assignment to avoid or defuse most of the potential problems while having fun with those present.

✦ Don't do anything that could make people feel self conscious or uncomfortable, including the onlookers.

✦ Don't allow specific personal contact, like breakfast, lunch, or coffee with the same guest to become a recurring thing.

✦ Don't consistently follow participation in an organized activity—like playing bridge, table tennis, or dance class—with an activity like lunch, coffee, or a stroll around the deck with the same lady.

✦ Don't work with the same lady in each dance class.

✦ Don't take seats down in front, especially if you're with a guest. Remember that the guests always come first. Hosts sit at the back of the rooms.

✦ Don't repeat any action or behavior with anyone that could be converted into an expectation. That is just what people will do. Unfulfilled expectations cause disappointment, anxiety, and frustration for the holder of them. Guests don't like the word no when you and the ship have taught them to expect something else. Don't be the cause of those disappointments.

✦ Don't join a lady in the hot tub more than once.

✦ Don't interrupt or pursue a lady who is present with an escort. She's not unaccompanied and not among the group of guests that a host should approach or invite to dance.

✦ Don't force or coax a lady to dance who has indicated that she's not interested at that time. She'll let you know when she's ready to dance.

The guiding rule is that a host must do with everyone what he does with any one specific lady. Be aware of the pitfalls listed above. Avoiding them with style and grace of a cultured gentleman will keep you free of entrapment and the appearance of partiality. Staying above envy, entrapment, and gossip while getting to know the guests and cheerfully doing your part within the framework of the host program is all there is to being a successful host. Done well, being a host is perhaps the most fun and rewarding activity a man can do.

Chapter 36 - ENDING THE CRUISE

● Preparation

Five days before an assignment ends and you leave your incredible temporary home, think through the things that need to be done before disembarking. Be sure that you'll have time for organizing and packing everything, old and new. If having the laundry done is one of the activities, get it done early enough for it to be returned. Collect any personal items loaned out, and return anything you checked out of the library. Discard all those things you can live without since packing space will be important. Or, see if the guest shop has any luggage left. Double-check the accuracy of your onboard financial account. With these things done, packing should be a simple process. It's my primary activity the last day of an assignment. I've said my goodbyes, and I'm not under pressure to get anything done. Other people like to start this process earlier.

● Thank You's

Be sure to thank everyone! Gifts are not necessary. You might pick up some thank-you notes along the way to write and send to those you've actually befriended.

Send these, exchange addresses, and finish other wrap up activities before the Captain's farewell party. Waiting until the last day of the cruise can produce disappointments. Even the regulars are often too tired or busy to show up that last night. Always have some of your business cards with you. Pass them out and get the ones you want from others well before the end of the cruise. Give out your hugs and goodbyes the night of the Captain's farewell party. Don't leave these exchanges for the last minute because they just won't happen that last day or night.

Make any farewells to the staff brief and in advance of the last day. You can bet that they're as anxious to rest and relax in their own space on that last day as the guests are to finish packing. Disembarkation day is also a busy embarkation one for the crew. On a ship, the staff has only a few hours to wish everyone goodbye and get the entire vessel ready before welcoming aboard the next group of guests.

● **Disembarkation**
When you're staying onboard, doing back-to-back cruises, you may be asked to assist passengers in one way or another. If you're uninvolved and choose to get up early in the morning to drift through the public areas, be ready to wish everyone well. Help them feel comfortable about the long day lying ahead of them. Some will be apprehensive about their flight(s) not to mention about getting through the airport(s). Many will regret the end of their adventure into this remarkable world. A thoughtful comment or two coupled with a compassionate smile can help shift their thoughts to the dreams of doing it all again.

All too soon it will be over for you too. When you disembark, remember that it's advantageous for your behavior to remain that of a host. As you reach the airport to begin flying home, the world you left behind will be waiting for you. Opening the door to your home, it will be back to doing your own grocery shopping, dealing with traffic, and the off-stage lifestyle you had left behind. After recovering from the adjustment, based on your exposure to the opportunities of hosting, you may be motivated to jump into a new dance or personal development program. You may be motivated to undertake private instruction to improve all sorts of things related to hosting and traveling the world. For everyone intent on living this life, there are skills that can always be developed before heading out on another assignment.

Chapter 37 - SUMMARY

I hope you're excited about having fun exploring the world in exchange for a bit of dancing. It's a real opportunity waiting to be savored by those who've invested the time in learning to be a good ballroom dancer.

Once you're comfortable with your dancing ability, you should turn that investment into receiving the payoffs that come from this unique business. The secrets, beyond the basic requirements, for those of you wanting to receive the richest rewards as one of those gentlemen selected for the good opportunities, were sprinkled throughout this book. While some were clearly emphasized, many were simply lying there for you to pick up. I hope that you got the ones needed in order to find the success that is rightfully yours as a host either on land or at sea. Appendix I provides information on certification should you be interested in my help getting started or improving your recognition as a host.

May your life be full of the rewards that this activity has to offer. I wish you smooth sailing, exciting new friendships, applause as a dancer and warm sunny weather as you live this lifetime.

May You Live Your Dreams

Appendixes

vanLee Hughey

APPENDIX I - DANCE HOST CERTIFICATION

CERTIFICATION SEMINAR:

For men wanting to get involved in Dance Hosting, seminars are usually conducted for groups of ten men or more on an as needed basis either in Atlanta or at facilities around the world. Since the objective is to certify each attendee for assignment, each participant must provide written certification of his ability to dance as discussed in section II of this book, DANCING AS A HOST. Accordingly, each person's danceability will be assessed in conjunction with the application of the social skills discussed herein - their personality. Dance pointers and social tips gained from this workshop setting will be invaluable in your cruise ship or any other dance setting.

Beyond the dance practicum is the critical information you will learn on selecting the type of assignment preferred and what happens after the successful application process. There are several different segments to this business each with its own advantages and disadvantages. That's important since there is a wide range of interest in any group of men. While working at my previous career, I could never have accepted several of the appointments that I relish today. I was limited to a different segment of the activity.

Armed with that information, each person who is prepared to submit an application to the proper agent or group is assisted in the preparation of their packet which should most definitely include a copy of their seminar certificate. Each person will have at least the clear mental road map needed to evaluate subsequent assignment offers. The details of each map varies by segment of the business to which one applies.

Additionally, each attendee will leave with recommendations on how to improve, where appropriate, any identified weaknesses.

Mail inquiries of space availability in pending seminars to:

      to: DanceMasters   or   E-mail: DanceMasters@att.net
         PO Box 95081   Subject-Dance Host Seminar
         Atlanta, GA 30347

Agents,   For host ratings, recommendations, or scheduling
Businesses,   seminars e-mail: DanceMasters@att.net
Dance Studios

vanLee Hughey

APPENDIX II - SUGGESTIONS FOR DANCE INSTRUCTORS

Normally, the resident instructors are a couple who are responsible for providing complimentary group lessons on the various ballroom dances for the guests. This role can be expanded in several different ways. For example, when there is a dance-host program, the instructors are often responsible for its effective operation. There may also be the opportunity or requirement to perform periodically as part of the evening entertainment. The instructors may be permitted to teach privately at their normal fee.

When you are considering an opportunity to become a resident instructor, make sure each of these areas and other responsibilities are defined as well as the salary and living arrangements. Review section IV for other issues to ask about. The role of the resident instructor is typically broader aboard the elite cruise ships than at resorts. However, a good resort will capitalize on a capable performance and instructing team. In all cases, the team is treated on a par with the hosts.

An instructor's preparation for an assignment is not that much different from that of a host. When performing is part of the assignment, the wardrobe is automatically expanded by the costumes in addition to related supplies like make up, music, videos, and a portable sound system.

In the elegant world we work in, the people interested in ballroom dance instruction are typically looking for a well-organized and usable lesson that's fun. Each session needs to be light-hearted and entertaining, but not silly or unusable that night. Here are a few suggestions that have produced great evaluations for many of these teams.

Sound System

Be sure that whatever sound system is to be used is working properly before the time class begins. Get there early and check it out each time! In some places the facility's technical staff has patched my little boom-box into the room's sound system and shown me how to adjust the sound. I ask specifically how to adjust the microphones reverb setting at that time. Often the size of the room and number of people attending the classes have warranted the use of a microphone.

A corded mike is a nuisance. Its cord will end up wrapped around someone's feet. I've also watched instructors struggle with cordless mikes; they were just in the way a lot of the time. I prefer carrying three complete wireless mikes, one for each person, and a spare. That way I'm using equipment that's familiar and my hands are free. All the facility has to do is make the connection to the sound system. I wear the cord and the transmitter inside my outfit to keep them out of the way. It's embarrassing to demonstrate a turn when your partner hooks your exposed wiring and flips the transmitter clipped on your waist up into never - never land with you attached.

Whichever mike is used, it often goes through a sound system set up for the band with reverb turned on. Don't let that happen to you. Be sure the reverb function is turned off at the console for the class.

Preparing for the Class

Each class is scheduled and announced in the printed program that everyone will use to arrange their day. For that matter, the only notification you may get is finding it in your copy of the program. Allow that, with your names, to suffice. Don't announce in the program what you'll be teaching. Be experienced and sharp enough to assess the needs of those who arrive to select the material appropriate for the group. If you're expecting a recurring group, as would be the case on a cruise with several sea days, it's a great idea for the first session to be something that will not intimidate the men who show up. When the guys are comfortable with what they have to do the first session or two, there's a good chance they'll return regularly thereafter. Intimidate the guy and the couple will never be seen again, and good luck with their evaluation! This problem is minimized on seven-day Alaskan or Caribbean cruises with only one or two sea days for lessons. It is, however, a significant problem on twelve-day crossings with six or more consecutive sessions. Even when there are mostly couples, if you help the men become comfortable early on, there's a good chance they'll return and their assessment of you will be the best possible. After the first class or two, what to teach at each session will become more dependent on who shows up.

Merengue has been used very effectively for the initial class for a six-or-more lesson cruise because its footwork is simple and not fast. Its patterns are equally simple for everyone to learn, and there is a lot of stimulating music that helps make this ice-breaker session feel good. This helps everyone get acquainted without concern about the dance they're doing since it is executed in a specific sequence called by the instructor. What's most important when the 45-minute class is done is that everyone has a minute merengue routine to dance. Get to know the band leader and let him/her know what is being taught each day so they can help support your work.

If each of the classes follows this basic structure, with a bit of light-hearted humor thrown in that is not offensive to anyone, people will keep coming back and will even knock on your door for private instruction. They'll also sing your praises to everyone they meet. To achieve this outcome across the spectrum of the ballroom and Latin dances takes preparation. The selection of music with slower-than-usual tempos is essential, since these are nondancers and barroom folks wanting to learn.

With this general outline in place, here's a laundry list of what works for me:

I. For each of the dances, my partner and I clearly know the patterns to be taught with virtually no surprises appearing in class. Even the jokes are normally rehearsed.

    A. Acknowledge if need be, but don't talk about or demonstrate other variations. Just teach the patterns in sequence. I attended a class on a long cruise where the instructors started teaching toe-heel swivels in swing. Everyone practiced them for fifteen minutes, but never with a partner. They then went into swing pinwheels which are unrelated to the swivels. Never, during the class or the remaining ten days of the cruise, did they return to toe-heel swivels. Other similar things in classes left everyone puzzled and generally confused.

    B. Don't teach the background or origin of the dance or its technical execution. This is a social dance class to help people have fun learning to do something today that they can use on the dance floor tonight. It isn't a dance theory, ballroom studio or competitor's prep class. Just help them learn to dance the

135

pattern(s) and eliminate the filler. Don't chatter to hear yourself talk! It's okay to be quiet when waiting for something, like the music to start.

C. When you've finished teaching the day's material, or when the allotted time is up, thank everyone for attending and then end the class. Do everyone a favor and say, "that's all folks," just once. Have you ever attended a class where the instructors brought it to a timely close, and then had a great idea, and decided they needed to teach just one more new pattern? Talk about frustrating and confusing everyone! Finish the instruction smoothly, leaving everyone three to five minutes to practice what they've learned. This short block of practice (or escape) time is more valuable to those in attendance than one more pattern pushed at them in non-existent class time.

II. Teach a maximum of four patterns, and then only if the guests can dance them. Normally, they'll be able to learn and dance successfully through three patterns in sequence by the end of the allotted 45 minutes. Teach, drill, and have them dance the patterns as a routine. That makes it easier for them to recall the material.

A Don't teach patterns that take more floor space than is available.

B. Don't teach patterns that are too difficult for them to actually accomplish in the time available. As instructors you're expected to know material and recognize that you're not working with students, dancers, or competitors. These are wonderful folks on vacation. They're here to have a good time, feel important, and get something that they may do later that evening on the dance floor. Those who will want to learn the advanced things will make arrangements for private sessions to learn them. That is where advanced material should be taught to those who want and can handle it.

III. Know what is going to be taught and decide who is going to teach the class.

A. Don't discuss what comes next. Teach one pattern and then the next.

B. Don't discuss or demonstrate what could be done or take time dancing your thing that isn't the pattern of the moment, etc. You're wasting everyone's time trying to impress them with your greatness. More importantly, it will confuse them.

C. Don't discuss and demonstrate something you're not going to teach them.

D. Don't remember a neat, nifty pattern, or variation and just toss it in ad-lib. You'll do enough of that along the way, which should be seamless to the class.

IV. There should be only one instructor during the class.

A. There should be only one instructor and that person does the teaching. He or she should ask for the partner's input when it's appropriate, otherwise, anything the other one has to say may be experienced as an interruption. There is no excuse for both to be talking at the same time, yet it happen frequently. It's as discourteous to the instructor and those trying to listen as it would be in any other social or professional situation.

V. Stop instruction at 40 minutes, make any last-minute comments, and use five minutes for them to practice while you provide any personal instruction that you didn't get to do during the class.

A. Don't run overtime. There are other functions and some folks will want to be on time for one of them.

B. Don't be generous and give them more than their money's worth. Just help them get it right. Too much is simply too much. That's neither usable later nor enjoyable now for at least some of the guests.

C. Don't discourage or embarrass anyone.

VI. Use a remote-control CD player or have a partner in place to make it work smoothly when wanted.

A. Know your music and have it ready before any class begins.

B. Have it preset to the right listening level, and selected for the ability of the people being taught.

VII. Teach by clearly and accurately walking through both the man's and lady's pattern so they understand what they're going to do.

A. Have either the men or the women practice their part first; then the other group, then see if they can do their parts separately at the same time. Correct it here until it's right enough to be doable.
B. Have them partner up and try it as couples; then redo this teaching sequence from the top (A.) if necessary to correct problems in one group at a time.
C. Keep moving. This is not the time to work with a specific couple or individual since the other people are ready to move on. Work with those in trouble during the practice period after the formal instruction.
D. Don't leave one group waiting too long; it will cause them to get bored and walk out. There is some logic for splitting men and women into two groups when there are two adequate and totally separate floors available in the same immediate area. Then, each partner of the teaching team gets their turn to do their thing with their group. However, when the group comes back together, there is just one instructor.

VIII. The instructor must always take time to be clear to the entire group about where it is in what pattern that he/she wants them to start, and then properly count them in.
A. When calling an execution sequence, do it far enough in advance that the group can hear it and the men can prepare to lead it properly.
B. The instructor should always provide a sufficient countdown (quick, quick, slow or 5,6,7,8 as appropriate) before having the group begin movement whether separated or partnered. They can't guess when you are going to start the execution or what tempo you are going to use. You've got to communicate that.
C. With or without music, instructors should always know the dance they're teaching well enough to count down in rhythm and start execution on the proper beat. When music is being used, the count down and start of execution should agree with the phrase of the music being played. For example, there is an eight-beat phrase in tango, a six-beat phrase in waltz, and cha-cha breaks on two with the schools starting it with a prep-step

on one. Count down and start each pattern on the proper beat of the phrase.

vanLee Hughey

INDEX

vanLee Hughey

FIGURES, FORMS AND PHOTOGRAPHS

vanLee Hughey

PERSONAL TRAVEL DIARY

---

vanLee Hughey

NOTES AND REMINDERS

vanLee Hughey

CONTACTS AND ADDRESSES

Name _____

Address _____

City, State, Zip _____

Telephone _____ E-Mail _____

Description _____

_____

Name _____

Address _____

City, State, Zip _____

Telephone _____ E-Mail _____

Description _____

_____

Name _____

Address _____

City, State, Zip _____

Telephone _____ E-Mail _____

Description _____

_____

Name _____

Address _____

City, State, Zip _____

Telephone _____ E-Mail _____

Description _____

_____

ABOUT THE AUTHOR

vanLee Hughey is actively traveling the world as a dance host with private groups as well as luxury cruise lines and a cabaret-style ballroom dancer when at home. He has performed successfully in major ballroom competitions, danced at major studios in the southeastern United States, hosted, taught on cruise ships since 1989, and is the owner of DanceMasters dance and training studio.

At the insistence of one of his students who was plagued by life long neuromuscular dysfunctions he formalized an effective coordination development program. He taught this Dance Therapy as a regular part of Emory University's community course schedule. While his dance work has included light opera as a singer/dancer, his hosting has landed him on the Phil Donahue Show.

By 1996, Lee knew that he'd rather be dancing on the oceans of the world instead of adding other plaques to his wall of data processing and leadership successes. An early retirement opportunity from the Centers of Disease Control and Prevention in Atlanta, Georgia made the major life change possible—opening the door to a life undreamed of by most.

Printed in the United States
1540100005B/37-39